DRIVING ITALY

A CHEEKY TRAVEL MEMOIR

RADA JONES

APOLODOR PUBLISHING

APOLODOR

DRIVING ITALY

OUR JOURNEY

1

THE BIRTHDAY WALK

Rada on her birthday contemplative walk. Like the one last year when she decided to get a dog. Me in the apartment writing a travelogue as she insisted.

God help us all! You have a sedative ready for her next idea?

I'M RADA. I'm a retired ER doc turned writer. I travel with my husband, Steve, a retired water and wastewater engineer. His motto is, "It may be sh@#t to you, but it's my bread and butter." He's the one left in the apartment to write the travelogue.

He's messaging to commiserate with our son, Tim, who recommended the sedative. For reasons yet to be determined, Tim, who loathes snow, lives in Buffalo, New York, which gets about as much snow as Alaska.

He shares his home with a dog who made her debut in a previous work of mine, a German shepherd named Guinness. Guinness Van Jones, to be precise. I named her after the show-stopping K-9 character in *Mercy*, my second ER thriller.

The final family member, the one who keeps us all in line, is Paxil. Paxil is deaf and black. She's also a cat, and she's very secretive about her age. Maybe because she doesn't hear us when we ask. But, since it's been sixteen years since we adopted her from the Humane Society, even if you hate math, you can figure that she's got to be at least sixteen.

She lost her hearing a few years ago after a botched ear cleaning (at the vet), but that doesn't bother her one bit. If anything, she naps better. She may still startle when Guinness wakes her up, but that doesn't faze her in the least. Guinness is Paxil's fourth German shepherd, and she's trained her well. She'll even steal her food at the risk of getting licked.

After we retired, Steve and I downsized from our lovely home on Lake Champlain to a three-season Adirondack camp the size of a school bus. And, since our simple abode is unfit for the North Country winters, we decided to spend this winter exploring the sunny shores of the Mediterranean, trying the diet and checking the wines — solely for health reasons, of course. We also planned to look for a sunny *pied-à-terre*.

We left Paxil and Guinness to look after Tim — they have joint custody of all of us — and flew to Paris. Two days later, I left the boys grumbling and took my usual long birthday walk to ponder the passage of time and think about my life, my past, and my future.

This was the birthday I officially graduated from middle age into being a senior, and we're in the middle of a pandemic, so I envisioned a momentous epiphany that would fill me with wisdom.

I left Steve home — he's not prone to epiphanies — and I went to *Pere Lachaise*, arguably the world's best-known cemetery. What better place to contemplate life's meaning and death's eternity than a cemetery, I thought. Especially this one, where so many VIPs would rub shoulders, should they be able to rub anything at all. *Pere Lachaise* is a who's-who of dead celebrities from Heloise and Abelard, Balzac, Bizet, Maria Callas, Chopin, Giacometti, Jim Morrison, and Edith Piaf to Oscar Wilde. There are more — the cemetery sells a map of their gravesites — but for the sake of brevity, I'll stop here.

Hoping that physical exhaustion would make me more prone to revelations, I walked the five miles from our Paris digs to *Pere Lachaise*. It took a while; by the time I got there, I was ready for a nap. But I stayed true to my mission. Instead of lying in the shade on one of the benches, I wandered pensively along the narrow alleys to gawk at famous people's eternal homes.

I saw tombs. Many tombs. Some brand spanking new, some old, some well-kept, some forgotten, some well-marked, some downright mysterious. It turns out that graves come in more flavors than gelato.

The one thing they all had in common was that they contained dead people. Rich or poor, kind or obnoxious, famous or obscure, their inhabitants were all dead. One would hope.

I wandered from tomb to tomb, seeking their wisdom. I quieted my brain and focused on the flow of my breath, struggling to ignore my growling stomach and opening myself to eternity.

Did I put the milk in the fridge?

I pushed back the errant thought and forced myself to meditate. I reminded myself that the better part of my life had already passed. What did I do with it? How did I change the world for the better?

I did the laundry. It should be dry by tonight.

Darn monkey brain! I shook my head to reset it and went back to pondering eternity. What an uphill battle!

The only thing that came to me is that once you're dead, nothing else matters. It doesn't matter if you were young or old, male or female, a sweetheart or an ice-hole. Not even if you did the laundry. Once you die, you die. Better make the most of everything while you're alive.

But that wasn't the epiphany I was longing for. Not even close. Maybe the famous tombs will inspire me, I thought, so I followed Mr. Google's directions to find them.

The pouty Egyptian angel guarding Oscar Wilde's marble tomb isn't happy. He doesn't like the plexiglass wall the family built to protect it from being defaced by lipstick kisses.

Edit Piaf moved back in with her parents. After a glamorous life of wild success and terrible heartbreak, her eternal quarters are so modest they're almost impossible to find.

Modigliani's concrete-covered slab is so worn it's hard to read. After his bust was stolen, Jim Morrison's grave was surrounded by an iron fence to stop his fans from drowning it in love letters, booze bottles, and pot.

I shuffled from one of the extinct great people to the next, attempting to think great thoughts. Something enlightening, having to do with the ephemerality of the flesh, the vanity of fame, and death's implacable permanence.

The only thing that came to mind was lunch.

I gave up. I guess the magic age of wisdom isn't sixty. Not for me.

I headed back.

I stopped along the way to wolf down a bowl of Pho. That's a fragrant Vietnamese soup loaded with meatballs, beef tripe, fresh mint, and rice noodles. That helped.

On a whim, I popped in on a hairdresser for a much-needed haircut. The lady who helped me was reasonably friendly and exceedingly meticulous. She trimmed a little to the left, some to the right, a bit more to the left, then some more to the right to make it even. By the time I left the hairdresser, I was half a pound lighter.

When I got home, Steve's worried eyes took me in. I don't know what he expected, but it wasn't good.

"Anything?" he asked.

"I got a haircut."

"That's it?" He breathed a sigh of relief.

"You like it?"

He shrugged.

"It will grow."

2

PARISIAN SNIPPETS OFF THE BEATEN PATH

OUR PARIS APARTMENT is tucked behind the Louvre, an hour-long taxi ride from Orly, and it's more of a studio than an apartment. You enter through the bedroom after fumbling up three dark floors of uneven steps smelling like local cooking, mold, and cats. But its tall windows look over the bustle of the café terraces that crowd the sidewalk. It has a coffee maker, a microwave, and more room than our cabin. And, unlike our house in the middle of the woods, this place is in the middle of everything!

One-minute walk to the pharmacy where 30 euros and a negative Covid test bought us three-day health passes allowing us inside restaurants and museums. Follow your nose to the smell of freshly baked bread for another minute, and you'll join the long line of the local *boulangerie*, where mouth-watering baguette sandwiches rub shoulders with luscious desserts too pretty to eat. One more minute and you're at the *Francprix*, a tiny convenience store that has everything from fine wines to toilet paper.

That's why I love Paris: Within a five-minute walk, you can find anything you want. Bus stops, cafés, Myanmar protest monuments, ATMs, and even the Louvre. Anything but a SIM card.

We wandered for hours before we found a small electronics shop where the TV blasted the Muslim call to prayer, subtitled in English and French. The helpful shopkeeper interrupted his worship to sell us a 50GB SIM card. He even installed it on my phone, allowing us to navigate, Google, and do whatever French people do with their phones.

Exhausted but accomplished, we dragged our jetlag back home. We sat by the windows to watch Paris, listen to the commercial-free French Radio's moody tunes, and sip on a fine Bordeaux.

This isn't our first time in Paris. We've been here many times before, running from the Orsay to the Louvre, checking out the Pompidou, and climbing the Eiffel Tower, but it was different this time. We hadn't come to visit; we'd come to live like the French. So we did. We walked the freshly washed side-walks until our feet hurt. We stopped for escargots in garlic butter, well-seasoned beef tartare, and crisp red Sancerre at the ubiquitous sidewalk cafés. We loitered in the parks to watch the kids play, the young people work out, and the elderly indulge in that most French of arts — the conversation. We breathed in the falling leaves' scent, soaked in the October sun, and napped in the Tuileries' comfortable metal chairs.

So we skipped the Louvre and the *Tour Eiffel*, but we visited the catacombs.

In the 1800s, Paris was running out of space. Its cemeteries took up so much real estate there was no space left for the living. Then the bloody French Revolution brought a new influx of dead, making it urgent to find a solution. The French, pragmatic as ever, did. They exhumed the city's cemeteries and turned the labyrinthine stone quarries underneath into a city of the dead, piling the dried bones in the quarries to free the land.

That made room under the sun for the living and provided a cozy shelter for the rest. Somewhere under Paris, the bones of Voltaire, Marat, Robespierre, and many other heroes who gave France her glory hang out with those of another seven million dead. And, since nobody knows who's who, the French venerate every broken skull, humerus, and femur like it belongs to a *Pater Patriae* (literally, Father of the Country).

After the catacombs, we walked along the Seine Quays, where, for centuries, the washing women used to do the Parisians' laundry, risking their lives every time the weather turned bad. And if you think they worked for the rich, you're mistaken. The Seine was too dirty for the rich. They sent their laundry to the countryside, where the water was cleaner.

Doing laundry in the Seine was recently outlawed, but the business remained. Hundreds of *lavanderies* along the Seine will still wash and iron your shirt for a couple of euros, even less if you subscribe. I don't know about you, but the thought of an ironing subscription leaves me cold. The last time I ironed something, it was money. I'm not really into money laundering, but these were all scrunched from sitting folded inside my money belt.

One beautiful October Sunday, we walked the four miles to the *Musée Marmottan Monet*, the previous spectacular home of Mr. Marmottan. We feasted our eyes on the great collection of Monet paintings and wondered at their grace and light. Then, tired but fulfilled, we headed back, looking for a place to have lunch. But there was none.

Restaurant after restaurant and café after café turned us down. Weary waiters shooed us off like a swarm of annoying flies. *On est complet,* they barked. We're fully booked.

C'est impossible ! Unfathomable, I thought, until I realized it was Sunday. That's when the French — apparently ALL the French — take their family out for lunch. So, if you don't have a family or at least a reservation, you're out of luck.

We walked and walked until our backs hurt, our stomachs growled, and our feet wore off. We walked until we fell upon a place that told us to seat ourselves. That should have been a warning, but we were too hungry to care.

It took hours to order and more hours to get our food. By the time the breadbasket arrived, Steve had finished his mediocre escargots, and I was done with my cold steak. But we'd warmed up with wine and rested our feet.

We eventually dragged ourselves home, but don't forget: No Sunday lunch in Paris without reservations.

Another day we went to see Notre Dame, though it was still closed after the tragic fire. We elbowed our way between the tourists and gawked over the fence at the ongoing reconstruction, ignoring the smoky gargoyles' ugly glares. That's how we discovered that the relics saved from the fire were displayed at the Paris architecture museum.

The statues of the twelve apostles used to live in the spire, but, thanks to God or good luck, they'd been removed to be restored just days before the fire. Now, they're all that's left from the doomed spire, other than the rooster weathervane. He may be a bit smoky and seriously gnarled, but he's still showing off his twisted tail. The three holy relics inside it that are thought to have saved him are back in the cathedral.

After Notre Dame, we visited *Sainte-Chapelle* to bathe our souls in its heavenly light. This jewel-like, stained-glass cathedral was built 800 years ago to host the Crown of Thorns brought to France by King Louis IX, Saint Louis to his many fans.

In those days, building a cathedral was the work of generations. *Notre-Dame de Paris* took ninety-seven years to complete. *Sagrada Familia*, Barcelona's pride, was started in

1882, and 141 years later, it's still in the works. *Sainte-Chapelle* took only ten years.

We pondered the essence of things in Brâncuși's stark workshop near the Pompidou. Driven by his passion for wood carving, Constantin Brâncuși, a Romanian shepherd, walked the two thousand miles from his home in Hobița to Paris. He started as an apprentice in Rodin's workshop but left two months later. "Nothing can grow in the shadow of big trees," he said.

He spent his life exploring the essence of things. That's how he created the most stylized sculptures the world had ever seen. He bequeathed his workshop to France, his adoptive country, provided that everything stayed unchanged. And it did. Stop by and visit. It's a low concrete structure right across from the Pompidou, and it's free. Everything inside looks like Brâncuși just stepped out to buy a baguette.

Paris was fun. It always is. But as the old Romanian saying goes, "The traveler looks better on the road."

Time to go. Normandy, here we come!

3

LEAVING PARIS

I DON'T KNOW MUCH about being homeless. Still, I can tell you that gathering all your belongings in a car to drive into the unknown is deeply unsettling.

After only ten days in Paris, I'd gotten used to "*la vie Parisienne*." We had "our" *Francprix*, "our" *boulangerie*, "our" favorite restaurant, "our" pharmacy. We'd built the beginning of a life, and that felt comfortable and comforting.

Leaving it to drive away was not, especially since we hadn't yet met "our" new car. We called it Rocinante.

Steve will tell you all about it since cars are his interest and one of his areas of expertise. But I'll give you a few basics:

1. It's big. It would be big anywhere, but here, on the five-hundred-year-old cobbled streets with even older parking spaces, it's humongous.

2. It's black. That wouldn't be a problem if all the other cars weren't black too. That tends to get confusing, especially for someone like me who doesn't see cars. I mean, I see them; I just don't pay attention. One time, a silver SUV stopped by as Guinness and I were walking to our cabin. I knew Steve was picking us up, so I opened the back door and urged Guinness in.

She hesitated, allowing me to see the horrified faces of the unknown driver and her daughter. They'd stopped to ask for directions and must have thought they were getting highjacked.

Another time, I finished shopping and went to unlock my car. I couldn't. I tried again, but the key didn't work. That's when I noticed the driver inside staring at me in horror. Oops! I smiled, waved, and made myself scarce before he called the police. So there.

I don't see cars because they don't interest me — unless they happen to be Lamborghinis. But, in case you're wondering, I'm not universally oblivious. I may not see cars, but I see people. I see their chins, and I can spot a difficult intubation across the parking lot. I see the white of their eyes, and I notice if it's yellow from jaundice, white from anemia, or red with conjunctivitis. Or if their thyroid is too big and needs checking. By their hands and the shape of their fingers, I know what sort of arthritis they have. I watch how they walk, and I know if they hurt. I also see dogs, cats, horses, landscapes, flowers, food, and wine. But cars? They're Steve's problem.

3. It has special red plates. Yay! Even I can see those. Advantage me! Also, advantage to the other drivers, who'll keep away if they have any sense.

4. Gwendolyn, the GPS, is the most stupid AI we have ever met. She couldn't find her mouth with a funnel since she has the IQ of a newt, but she compensates for it with her warm, soothing voice with a lovely British accent. Even her French pronunciation is better than mine, unlike Ms. Google's, our phone's GPS, whose French would give a Frenchman a seizure. But at least Ms. Google knows where she's going, while Gwendolyn couldn't find the Eiffel Tower if it fell in her lap.

She's industrious, though. Whenever I ask for directions, she has me choose between the fastest, shortest, or most ecological routes. But though she knows we're in Italy, it doesn't cross her artificial mind that if I ask for Doglio, I'm looking for the one 20 kilometers away, not for Dogli Street in Dublin. And she's spiteful, too. Whenever Steve ignores her instructions and gets us lost, she'll send us a few miles down the road to make a U-turn just to punish us.

5. Rocinante is a plug-in hybrid. But, like a true man, Steve didn't read the instructions. Neither did I — I don't drive, so they're not my problem. That's why we ran out of electricity half an hour into our trip. And gone, it stayed, until I broke down and read the instructions.

That should keep you going until you read Steve's take, and maybe even if you don't. Let's get to the driving…

Steve drives — that's what he does. He's American and a man, so he loves driving. Steve drives like birds fly, fish swim, and snakes slither.

I don't unless I must. Even then, I'd rather walk. It never crossed my mind to drive just for fun. I'll never forget my first American days when Steve and I were just getting to know each other.

"Let's go for a ride," he said.

"A ride to where?" I inquired.

"Just a ride."

"Yes, but to where?"

"To nowhere. Just to enjoy the landscape."

That got me worried. I wondered if he was sick. It took me years to understand that Steve goes for a ride like I go for a walk — for the fun of it.

That's why he drives and I don't.

But don't think I'm totally useless — I'm not. I do pretty much everything else: I navigate, translate, supervise, shop, and nag. I watch his right side since he's got a bunch of fused verte-brae, so he can't turn his head. And I suffer at least a minor heart attack whenever we're about to crash.

I had three of them during our first hour in the car. First, we took a one-way street the wrong way; then, we almost crashed into a bus. But the worst was when we almost lifted a woman off the pedestrian crossing as Steve struggled to find his turn signal. But I screamed, and he hit the brakes. I told you I was useful!

That first day took a few years off my life. We had a brand-new car we didn't know, way too big for the roads. There were all the new rules, new signs, and a new drivers' culture. And don't even get me started on the roundabouts!

I knew the French had a penchant for wine, cheese, and *bons-mots*. But I didn't realize they had a roundabout addiction.

Roundabouts are to the French what turning right on red is to Americans, U-turning to Thais, driving on the wrong side to Brits, and sitting on the horn to Indians in Mumbai. Every place has its share of driving quirks, and for the French, it's roundabouts.

They are EVERYWHERE, and drivers love them.

I came to believe that French drivers would rather go 450 degrees through a roundabout than take a right turn. I even spied a couple turning round and round, like in NASCAR, just to be social. Like weeds, the French roundabouts sprout every-where and come in every flavor. Some are entire landscaped parks, complete with statues and water features. Some are just black circles in the road, no bigger than a dinner plate. Some have only two exits — imagine that. One entry, one exit, and they make it into a roundabout rather than go straight. Some have up to seven exits, so you need to count out which one is yours, and we always get it wrong.

After getting off track again and again, we got into counting aloud together like kindergarteners. We still get it wrong because some of the would-be exits are not exits at all. They're driveways, parking lots, or just decoys intended to confuse us poor Americans.

But enough of that. If you want to know more about the car and lease options, read Steve's take. As for me, I'm on my way to Normandy. We head to Honfleur via Monet's garden in Giverny, where lily pad aficionados of all persuasions congregate to get their fix.

Car Rental: The Engineer's Take

Car rentals in Europe are generally similar to the U.S. Still, 2021's scourge of Covid, with its effects on travel, affected the automobile industry in several negative ways. Some rental companies had to sell off most of their fleet. Our go-to rental company, Hertz, reorganized under bankruptcy and had virtually no availability in Europe.

When Europe started reopening in the summer of 2021, the rental companies were unprepared for the associated demand. Many raised their rates to ridiculous levels as they tried to build back inventory.

French car manufacturers stepped into this void with a unique lease program. French car manufacturers Peugeot, Citroën, and Renault offer a particular long-term rental (or short-term lease) agreement under a "buy-back" program. The manufacturer "sells" the car to the lessee. They provide registration, insurance, and all other necessities for the lease period, then agree to buy back the vehicle at the end of the lease for the full price minus the lease payment.

A few U.S.-based agents coordinate these long-term car leases. We applied through Auto Europe, located in Portland, Maine, and submitted an online application for the smallest Peugeot available. The agent advised us that we were late (one month before arriving) and that the car we wanted won't be available until November. There were virtually no cars available for October.

They eventually found us a medium-sized — and more expensive — Citroën SUV. Instead of the US$3,000 for a small Peugeot for 161 days (5 months+), the larger Citroën would cost US$4,559 for the vehicle, registration, no-deductible insurance, etc.

We agreed. They confirmed our reservation, charged our card, and sent us "purchase" and "buy-back" agreements to execute.

There were multiple locations in Paris and throughout Europe for vehicle pickup, mostly at major airports. Still, since we would stay in downtown Paris for our first ten days, we arranged for a downtown pickup.

When the time came, we took an Uber for less than 25 Euros. We arrived at TT Transport fifteen minutes before our scheduled pickup to find everything ready. We went through the paperwork showing the car registered and insured in our names, then through a comprehensive orientation.

The vehicle was a brand-new Citroën C5 Aircross Hybrid, which was no surprise. The surprise was that it was also a plug-in similar to our Toyota plug-in hybrid at home. This plug-in hybrid has a 1.6-liter 180-horsepower turbocharged internal combustion engine coupled with an 80-kilowatt electric motor. The engine powers the front wheels through an 8-speed automatic transmission along with the electric motor. Sadly, this SUV, like most in Europe, does not have all-wheel drive.

The plug-in range is 50—60 kilometers in electric vehicle mode, and the car was delivered with the battery fully charged. We left the agency and drove in electric mode from Paris to Giverny while getting used to the car, which has a lot of displays and features that are somewhat distracting. Add to that the new roads and the French driving practices, and you'll conclude that it's fortunate the car came with bright red license plates in place of the usual white ones. The red plates warn the other drivers that this is a vehicle "in transit" and they should beware!

All the lease cars have GPS navigation, but the new system takes some getting used to. The information system includes Apple Car Play, which we often used with Google Maps or Waze when the built-in system couldn't find what we needed.

Some other features include lane departure warning, side obstruction radar, and front collision avoidance. There's also a parking assist radar and a 360-degree camera system that makes parallel parking a breeze. The car sports a panoramic sunroof, but the seats are only manually adjustable, not heated, and lack an adjustable lumbar support.

The C5 Aircross uses about 7 liters of petrol per kilometer driven in hybrid mode (about 34 miles per gallon), even better with plug-in charging. Each full charge gains about 50 kilometers of electric vehicle range before the ICE (internal combustion engine) kicks in. Unfortunately, electric charging while on a touring vacation is a challenging task. Each day usually involves much more driving than the EV (electric vehicle) range, and it's awkward to ask at a bed and breakfast for the use of an electrical outlet. Fast charging stations don't seem to like credit cards — they want a subscription or a smartphone app, so we found it easier to forget the plug and just operate as a hybrid vehicle.

We also found out the hard way that petrol stations are never located in France's small historical villages, so we ended up running under a low-fuel warning while searching for petrol (European for gasoline). Filling up should get easier as we get more used to the process. The ICE and motor/generator can also charge the battery and reserve a certain amount of EV range when you're down to petrol fumes.

4

MONET'S GIVERNY

JUST AN HOUR away from Paris's bustle, Giverny may as well be on the other side of the world. It's just a tiny village with sleepy little houses, well-loved gardens, and narrow streets that still struggles to come to terms with its fame.

It all started in 1883 when Monet, 43 years old and about to get famous, rented a house in Giverny to shelter his blended family. He fell in love with the place and never left. He spent his next 40 years there, painting, gardening, and bringing beauty to the world.

Monet, a rebel painter, decried by the time's critics for his "*plein-air*" (outdoor) painting, started a movement that would end up revolutionizing the art. Unlike the time's celebrated painters with their classic stuffy "salon" works, Monet's paintings were all about light and emotion. His ironic critics called it "impressionism," in the same vein as "exhibitionism" and "voyeurism." The name came from one of Monet's early paintings of a sunrise on the Seine, a dreamy blur of light and color he named "Impression — Soleil Levant."

The term stuck. So did the movement.

Monet thought he'd move on. But he didn't.

He spent his next forty-three years growing the gardens at Giverny and painting them. He brought water lilies from all over the world to plant in his pond, then spent day after day painting their light. As he grew old and his eyes faded, besieged by cataracts, his paintings grew larger and larger. His vision dimmed so much that he needed to label his paint tubes. But he never gave up.

Monet's last paintings, displayed in Paris at the *Musée de l'Orangerie*, are enormous and almost abstract, with a few water lilies every now and then. These massive windows to Monet's heart are all about water and light, the message of a half-blind Monet to a world forever changed by the First World War: Never give up.

Neither the sharp wind nor the hibernating gardens could deter us from stalking Monet's ghost along the shady paths. We pulled our windbreakers closer and picked up the pace, but we soaked in the light. We watched the sun's rays play on the water, and we bowed to Monet's genius in both painting and gardening. Then, frozen but inspired, we drove on.

5

HONFLEUR

Since we lived on Lake Champlain for years, with Quebec as
our backyard, we looked forward to seeing Honfleur, where it
all had started. But the tiny fishing village Samuel de Champlain left to settle in Canada and initiate Quebec is no more.
There's still some fishing if you believe the few remaining
fishing boats. But Honfleur's heated love affair with the impres-
sionists showered it in fame and made it a hot tourist attraction.
Its narrow streets with lousy parking were clogged with tourists
warming their hands on coffee cups, elbowing each other to
take selfies with the port, and buying local biscuits, cider, and
cheeses in fancy shops with fancier prices.

Hungry and tired, we hoped for a nice bistro dinner and a
glass of wine to warm us up. Easy, you'd think, since the place
was nothing but restaurants. Still, we drove round and round
but found no parking. So I left Steve to watch the car and went
hunting for a baguette or anything looking like dinner, but I
found nothing, so I settled for a bottle of calvados.

France may be the country of vineyards and wine, but
Normandy belongs to the apple orchards. Hence, its drinks of
choice are cider and calvados, which is a cider distillate.

Calvados takes years to smooth, and it's still an acquired taste, much like a single malt. But calvados is exactly what Normand cuisine needs. Normandy boasts rich, creamy sauces, ripe Camembert cheese, and seafood of all kinds, from the sweet raw oysters served with a splash of cider vinegar to stuffed warm mussels smothered in creamy bacon sauce and served with a generous pile of fries. Even its famous dessert features calvados — *Le Trou Normand* is a scoop of apple ice cream floating in a glass of calvados.

But after the first day of driving, in which our proudest achievement was not killing anyone, we were too exhausted to enjoy Honfleur's overpriced charms. We found our cheap hotel and had a takeaway Turkish kebab for dinner, washed down with calvados. The following day, weary but rested, we headed towards Bayeux, the city of tapestry fame and the gateway to the Normandy beaches.

6

BAYEUX

WE LOOKED FORWARD to seeing the famous Bayeux tapestry, but like many things in life, the tapestry wasn't quite what it was claimed to be. As a matter of fact, it's not even a tapestry. It's a 200-foot-long embroidery giving a blow-by-blow account (literally) of some of the remarkable eleventh-century happenings that made our world what it is today.

In 1066, following the death of the childless Edward the Confessor, the Anglo-Saxon king, his nephew William, the Duke of Normandy, gathered an army and crossed the channel to fight the incoming Anglo-Saxon King, Harold, for the crown.

The Normands of the time were slightly French, mostly Vikings, and totally warriors. These marauding descendants of Rollo had abandoned their Viking plundering boats to settle in Normandy just two hundred years earlier. Their horses, skilled archers, and superior strategy proved too much for the Anglo-Saxons. King Harold caught an arrow in the eye and died, making room for William to become king of England. That's how the Norman Conquest became a thing.

But for the Norman Conquest, England, as we know it

today, would not exist. Neither would English language, Shake-speare, roast beef, America, rugby, and warm beer. So there.

The tapestry, though very thorough, doesn't quite get to the warm beer. It ends with William's coronation, which is good because it's already long enough.

Our home in Bayeux turned out to be a quaint apartment with low sloped ceilings, an excellent view of the Bayeux roofs, a temperamental stove that took us two days to learn, and French-only speaking TV, but no heat or warm water. So, when the stingy October sun went down and the evening chill reached our bones, we curled under the covers to watch *The Longest Day* and prepare for our pilgrimage to the Normandy beaches. The following day, we took a Romanian bath — that's wiping yourself with a soapy towel — and, smelling riper than many Normand cheeses, we headed to the beaches.

7

NORMANDY

ON JUNE 6, 1944, the largest fleet the world had ever seen started the reverse invasion of the Norman Conquest. Thousands of soldiers, many just kids — American, British, French, Polish, Canadian, and others — sailed from England to liberate France and the rest of the world from Hitler's grasp. Thousands of them died at dawn, struggling to scale the German defenses.

They got mowed down by bullets, blown up by guns, shattered by mines, or drowned in the shallow waters. Hundreds of wounded bled to death on the beaches when they couldn't advance to find shelter, and their partners could not help them. It's a sacrifice, the magnitude of which blows the mind.

After hours and days of tremendous effort and pain, the allies broke through the German defenses and moved inland at a cost that makes me shiver. The endless forest of white marble crosses overlooking Omaha Beach goes farther than the eye can see. And every marble cross is not only a young life cut short. It's a family that never got to be whole again. I tried, but the loss is too immense to fully comprehend.

But France remembers. And so should we.

The monument on Omaha Beach is a stark reminder that freedom isn't free. It's horribly painful and terribly expensive. And, sadly, those who pay its price don't get to enjoy it. That's why the least we can do is be grateful and value our freedom, the priceless gift of thousands of heroes we'll never meet.

8

BRITTANY

OUR HEARTS HEAVY WITH LOSS, we left the beaches and headed south to Brittany, France's wild side. We skipped *Mont Saint-Michel*, the old Abbey sitting on a part-time island that Normandy and Brittany have disputed for hundreds of years, since we'd already been there. It can be awe-inducing if you can ignore the hordes of noisy tourists trampling over each other to take selfies on the ramparts, and the slew of fake-medieval outfits selling passable food and useless tchotchkes. But France has too much to see and do to waste your time and money on mediocre things you've already done. So we waved to it from afar and pushed on to Brittany.

Brittany was love at first sight. We took a right turn after Normandy and found ourselves looking over endless mudflats leading to the distant sea. Dozens of determined people wearing colorful raincoats and tall rubber boots carrying child-sized rakes and buckets braved the mud and filed toward the sea to look for oysters. A playful wind whipped our faces, filling our noses with the salty smell of algae, oysters, and dead fish. We passed shop after shop advertising "*la dégustation*" and whole-sales of *"huitres,"* (oysters,) *"moules,"* (mussels,) and other delicacies that only ever come in tiny portions. And just like that, I was hooked!

We drove north toward *Cap Frehel*, where a rugged rocky shoreline the color of old Bordeaux held firm against gusts of wind whipping it with lashes of freezing rain. Massive green waves chased each other to the shore to crash in exuberant spumes against the rock. The wind whistled, waterbirds screamed, and heavy raindrops struck my face, and I suddenly felt at home, though I'd never been here. There was something electrifying about this nature, letting loose so shamelessly. I laughed with delight as I climbed higher and higher on the wet slippery rocks dressed in green, yellow, and rust-colored moss. How fun!

Steve looked worried, but he waited patiently for me to come to my senses. That took a while, but we eventually drove on. Still, I kept stopping him. I couldn't get enough of all the part-time islands (like *Mont Saint-Michel*, they're only islands at high tide). Those crafty Bretons, hundreds of years ago, made the most of the handy setting. They fortified it into impregnable castles that looked like they grew from rock.

Once past the untamed Breton shore with its fortresses and lighthouses, we drove into its astounding agriculture: miles and miles of lush plantations of blue-green cabbage, fat leeks, and exuberant cauliflowers exploding with energy.

Truth be told, everything in Brittany vibrates with energy: the plants, the weather, and the people. Brittany is not France. Even though this wild peninsula has been part of France for hundreds of years, it still maintains its Celtic vibe and language. It has never stopped dancing to its own tune. That's highly unusual in France, a country that prides itself on being French first and everything else later. How come, you ask?

It all started with Anne, the Duchess of Brittany.

On September 9, 1488, Anne's father, Frances II, the Duke

of Brittany and the last male of the House of Montfort, fell off his horse and died without leaving a male heir. That left Anne, age 11, who'd already lost her mother, to inherit not only Brittany but a bunch of headaches she could do without.

Noble suitors of all nationalities, aged from babies to seniors, lined up for the young duchess's hand — and the hefty dowry. There were so many that her advisors couldn't agree on a suitor. Anne took off, leaving them to squabble. Still, on December 19, 1490, Anne, now aged thirteen, got married by proxy to Maximilian I of Austria, eighteen years her elder, whom she had yet to meet. He must have been busy.

But Charles VIII, the mighty King of France, was less than pleased. First, Anne's marriage without his consent violated the treaty he'd signed with her father. Second, these nuptials put Anne — and therefore Brittany — in the hands of France's powerful enemy. "Not only no, but hell no," he said, most likely in French, and decided to marry her himself.

That romantic approach did, however, present a few problems.

First, Anne was technically married, even though she hadn't met her husband. Second, it so happens that the king was married too. He'd been married to Maximilian's daughter, Margaret of Austria, for eight years. His wife, eleven years old at the time, had been brought up at the French court waiting for the couple to be old enough to consummate the marriage. And finally, Anne de Bretagne and Charles de France were closely related, and their consanguinity violated the rules of the Catholic church.

But Charles was a determined young man who wouldn't let such trivial things get in love's way. He asked the pope for an annulment to dissolve his marriage to Margaret of Austria, another annulment for Anne's marriage to Maximilian, and a dispensation to allow him to marry Anne. The pope was eager to please his powerful ally, so he granted Charles this "buy two get one free" deal. That's how the fourteen years old Anne of Brittany became Queen Consort of France, and Brittany became part of France.

What did Anne think about all this? I bet nobody asked her, but I don't think she liked it much. Documents say that she brought two beds instead of one when she came to her wedding with Charles and that the king and queen often lived apart.

But that didn't stop Anne from being pregnant throughout her marriage. Seven years later, she had had at least six pregnancies that did not produce living children. Anne was only 21 when Charles managed to hit his head against a marble door lintel in the palace of Amboise and died, leaving Anne a widow and returning Brittany to her.

Finally free? Not so much. Anne's nuptial contract to Charles stipulates that she must marry the heir of her dead husband, Louis, soon-to-be XII, to keep Brittany in France's fold. But Louis is not only Charles's second cousin; he's also his brother-in-law since he is married to Charles' sister, Joan.

Impossible? Mais non. The helpful pope comes through again with another annulment. One year later, Anne is Queen Consort of France once more.

But she's older and wiser, and her new husband loves her dearly. He consents to her requests regarding Brittany, allowing it freedoms that exist nowhere else in France. That's why, even today, Brittany's roads are still free. Brittany is the only place in France where highways have no tolls.

It's been more than five hundred years, but Anne's spirit still lives in Brittany. Her stained-glass portrait graces the cathedral *Basilique St-Sauvier* of Dinan, Brittany's capital. And to this day, Brittany's wild spirit, Celtic language and art, and even its cuisine set her apart from the rest of France.

Unlike the rest of France, you won't find baguettes in Brittany. You'll discover *galettes*, gray buckwheat crepes sold by the dozen that get filled with anything from seafood to fruit and become the Bretton's breakfast, lunch, and dinner.

The stone houses are tall and timbered, and they lean toward each other across the narrow streets like they want to steal a kiss from each other, but it's not love. It's all about money. Like much of Medieval Europe, Brittany's taxes were based on the ground floor surface area, so wise builders built wider at the top.

Our Dinan home was a tiny apartment that had started its life as a garage. It opened to a steep cobbled street so narrow that passing was out of the question. Moreover, to cut down on the traffic, the crafty locals placed plants and chairs by their doors, making the street almost impassable. To drop off the luggage, Steve had to fold the car's mirrors, and I had to walk ahead to guide him before parking half a mile away.

But it was no hardship to stroll up and down Dinan's cobblestoned streets to window-shop, soak in the atmosphere, and communion with the local cats. I had a blast.

Steve didn't. Once again, the oysters didn't agree with him, and we started wondering if he was developing a seafood allergy. What a pity that would be! The only thing worse would be being allergic to wine.

Still, we got to enjoy some funky folded galettes looking like origami, with prices to match, that looked way better than they tasted. We window-shopped all things sailing, from rigging to charts and designer foul-weather gear, without buying a thing. We walked St. Malo's old ramparts to watch students learn how to sail and listen to the school kids taking history and architecture classes up on the old city walls. It was a lovely time, but all good things must end. We left Brittany to drive to Bordeaux.

9

BORDEAUX

THERE'S nothing more French than Bordeaux, not even cosmopolitan Paris. Bordeaux vineyards are the magic place where the French tradition, esthetics, *joie de vivre*, discipline, sensuality, and pragmatism converge into wine.

The long, tidy rows of vines align like soldiers in formation as far as the eye can see, and they're glorious now that October has set them on fire. The grapes were harvested already, but there's still an errant cluster here and there that you can steal to touch, smell, and taste the glory of the *terroir*. That's what the French call their land.

To make the best wine, the vine has to suffer. No sissy things like irrigation here (it's outlawed). Water is a luxury you have to earn. That's why the dauntless roots grow deep into a soil of lime and clay that no American farmer would call fertile. They suck in the precious water and, with it, the exquisite aromas that make the Bordeaux wines unique. The hints of citrus, leather, chocolate, dark fruit, smoke, apricot, and violet are all flavors of the soil absorbed into the wine. They don't get added to the wine during the vinification process like one misguided tourist asked. I was pleased to see that the vintner didn't kill him.

After the torture of thirst comes the torture of torture. Every winter, the vines get pruned within an inch of their lives. They lose all their branches but one or two per plant that get twisted between guiding wires and forced into a flatness no vine ever imagined. And that's all before the picking, crushing, and fermenting of the grapes. The vine suffers. But that's the price the sun and land require to create the precious bottles of Jesus's blood that bring awe and joy to wine lovers all over the world.

Bordeaux's beating heart is in Saint-Émilion, a thousand-year-old village founded by Émilion, the Benedictine monk who became its patron. After he died in 876, he was sanctified for his life of asceticism and religious fervor. A bit ironic in a place that's all about sensuality and pleasure, don't you think? Still, his miracles are said to continue to this day. Women who want children should sit in Saint-Émilion's meditation seat — now called the seat of fertility — and they're guaranteed to become pregnant within the year. Does that work? Yes, say the hundreds of grateful birth announcements displayed nearby. I'm a skeptic, but I avoided that seat like the plague.

Hundreds of years ago, Saint-Émilion's faithful followers started the vineyards and shaped Bordeaux's future into tidy oak barrels.

But there's more to Saint-Émilion than wine. Deep below the city streets hides a whole city carved in limestone. That's where the quarries used to be that provided the stone for the majestic buildings in nearby Bordeaux and the countless local vineries, who all, from the smallest to the grandest, call themselves "*chateaux,*" castles.

One could easily get lost in the dark limestone labyrinth of caverns and corridors marred by the smoke of old candles. But you can't get there without the local guide who bursts with pride sharing the town's history and showing you the largest monolithic church in France.

The church, 38 meters long with a bell tower 68 meters high, is carved in limestone. It was dug in the 12th century out of a single block of stone — therefore monolithic — to complement the underground stone city.

These days, the quarries took on a new life. They are the city's wine caves. That's where, after the pain of fermentation, the magic of aging takes place. The new wines are sheltered in French oak barrels (Hungarian oak won't do, our guide said). They wait for years to mature before getting released from their oak prison to get bottled, then sent to awe the world. Depending on the vineyard and the year, a bottle of Bordeaux can cost more than a small house, garage included. Still, there's a wine for every budget. You can buy a nice Bordeaux for the price of a Belgian beer, if that's what you can afford.

To celebrate the vineyards — and save some money, since Saint-Émilion is not cheap — we stayed at a B&B in the vineyards. It had tall ceilings and massive windows opening over the golden rows of vines, but no TV or fridge and a limping Wi-Fi.

Madame Maryse, the owner, lived alone in her large house in the vineyards that must have been a *château* someday. She was delighted to chat with us in French and English as she fed us delicious continental breakfasts with warm baguettes and aromatic fruit preserves she'd made herself.

Without TV or the internet, we spent three days watching the colorful hot-air balloons float toward the sky at sunrise, reading old books, and walking around the *châteaux*. That's what the French call the homes of the wines, even those that look like garden sheds. To every *viticulteur*, his home is a castle.

We talked, not always kindly. When you're addicted to the

internet, not having the news at your fingertips is profoundly unsettling. You know that things are happening somewhere. Important things that matter to those you love and to you. Not knowing them hurts.

Our internet withdrawal got us shaky and short-tempered. Our nerves got frayed, and all tolerance went out the window. We had a big fight. Whatever it was, it felt earth-shattering. A week later, I couldn't remember what it was about.

The highlight of our stay in Saint-Émilion was our lunch at *Le Bis*, a restaurant with a thoroughly uninspired name that served us a meal to remember.

The variety of cheeses on display got me befuddled. There were green, yellow, white, and blue cheeses; hard and soft; speckled and marbled; moldy and holey; Normand, Bretton, Provencal, Dutch, Italian, Spanish or Basque. An orgy of cheeses like I'd never seen.

How do you even choose? I didn't.

I ordered the *foie gras* instead. It was earthy, unctuous, almost orgasmic, sprinkled with a few large grains of *Sel de Merlot* to enhance its smoothness. And boy, did it go well with the wine — Bordeaux, of course. That wine alone set us back 60 euros but bought us memories we'll never forget.

Warmed by the wine and encouraged by my success with the *foie gras*, I ordered the steak. The waitress frowned with worry. I was American, therefore, not to be trusted near French meat.

"How do you want it cooked?"

"*Saignant.*" Rare, I said, and she sighed with relief. I wondered why until I saw the chef light a handful of twigs for a fire, and I realized it was for the steak: "*L'entrecote sur les sermants de la vigne,*" beef steak cooked on burning vines. The fire was spectacular but short-lived. It didn't last long enough to boil a soft egg. That's when I noticed the note on the menu:

Steak served bloody or raw (!) with wild mushrooms, smashed potatoes, and shallots.

What an unforgettable day! So was the scent of that place that I'll forever think of as the scent of seduction: a subtle mix of charred meat, good wine, and expensive perfume with a touch of vine smoke. If I could bottle it, I'd get rich.

10

PROVENCE

IF BORDEAUX IS the epitome of perfect French order, with vines, bottles, and barrels aligned like soldiers in formation where nothing dares to defy the plan, from the fermentation temperature to how many times you can reuse an oak barrel, Provence is another kind of French.

Provence is wild, tortuous, and crazy. Its gnarled olive trees twist like black flames crowned by silvery-green leaves floating like smoke. Its in-your-face jagged mountains hide the horizon and stir your soul. Its white horses with long flowing manes fly over the marshes, and the narrow roads slither like black snakes under the trees. Provence is the France of sun, lavender, and garlic, the passionate land of the Mistral, Cezanne, and Van Gogh.

I can't but love Bordeaux's blood of the grapes and bow at its meticulous perfection, but Provence? I feel it in my bones, like arthritis.

That's why, when I had to decide on a place to spend our break from vacation, I chose Provence.

Why does a vacation need a break, you wonder? Good question.

First, this isn't exactly a vacation. It's a nomad lifestyle, and it comes with lots of work. A month after leaving home, I'm working on two books. I'm editing *Lovely K-9*, book 4 in my *K-9 Heroes* series, and I've started this still-to-be-named travel memoir. Between them, they take at least 3—4 hours of my day every day. And they require silence, inspiration, and Wi-Fi.

Second, changing domiciles every other day leaves you no time to settle. You don't get to learn your temporary home's quirks and learn your way around to find the best *boulangerie* or shop at the farmer's market. You have no time to dry your laundry, sit on a bench to study the locals, or even rest. You're just a traveler without a home.

That's why, after three weeks of changing home base every other night, we settled in Aix-en-Provence for nine days: to do laundry, catch up on work, and breathe.

We found our apartment on Home Exchange, a website where people exchange homes for vacations. I got in touch with the owner, but he wasn't excited to host us. I bet the only reason he took us on was my French. He found it entertaining.

We talked, we googled, and we emailed. We exchanged pictures of the window where he had hidden the key and learned where not to park. When all was said and done, finding the place looked about as likely as finding the Holy Grail, so I checked out the nearby hotels. Just in case.

Still, we made it. We found the unnamed street, the building, and even the window with the key hidden behind the grate. We unlocked the main door and discovered the mailbox that contained the following key. The one thing we didn't find was the apartment number.

We had a key to one of the six apartments in that building.

Logic has always been my strength. Our host's name was the one before the last on the owners' list, so maybe his place was on the upper floor? That only left two doors to try. That made it only a 50-50 chance that someone would call the police to throw us in jail.

After seven hours of driving with no toilet, I was ready to take my chances. They've got to have toilets at the police station, I thought. But Steve's genius came to bear. He planted his finger on the doorbell and sent me to listen from door to door. That's how we found our new home.

Living in someone's home is fascinating. It's more voyeuristic than looking into people's houses through lit windows, though not quite as bad as watching some reality shows. You don't get to see the people, but you get to see their lives: you eat from their dishes, sleep between their sheets, and read their books.

The most revealing thing is the fridge. You won't believe what you can learn about people by studying their fridge. And their pantry.

Our hosts didn't live in luxury, but their place was functional, well-organized, and meticulously tidy. The hundreds of labeled jars of spices packed tightly in white IKEA drawers within drawers would have warmed an OCD sufferer's heart.

They were into *bio* — the French word for organic — for everything, from yogurt to food wrappers to kombu. If you're not into kombu, that's a dry alga used to flavor Japanese cuisine. I'd never met any made of plastic.

They left us a thick file of instructions, from "don't bring the outdoor chairs inside because they scratch the floor" to the three-page description of troubleshooting the washing machine. All in French, of course.

Steve (who doesn't speak French) and I got to spend romantic moments bonding over exciting things like the internet password, turning on the TV, and taking out the bottles. The recyclables went two streets away, unlike the trash. That went at the end of our road.

Steve didn't like it. Living in someone else's space made him uncomfortable, so much so that I promised to get him a hotel room if he was still suffering in a couple days. He worried about spilling wine on the floor, damaging the wooden counters, and forgetting where to put which stuff. Me? I was too tired to care.

But it was worth it. We sat on the narrow terrace on the small hard chairs we didn't bring inside, inhaling the aroma of the neighbors' fresh laundry and drinking the Bordeaux we'd brought. We looked over the nearby gardens to the misty silhouette of *Montagne Sainte-Victoire* and toasted to Cezanne, the city's most famous son, who painted it until the day he died. And knowing that we wouldn't have to move again tomorrow felt good.

11

PROVENCE'S ARTISTS

No wonder Provence is all about art. Its harsh sun brings out colors things didn't know they had. There's no gray in Provence.

Paul Cezanne, Aix-en-Provence's favorite son and one of the forefathers of modern painting, said: "You want to know how to paint gray? You paint it with colors. Shade is another color, just less bright."

He spent years struggling to find the right nuances to paint his favorite subject, *Montagne Sainte-Victoire*. The humped rock triangle looming above Aix-en-Provence has become its symbol. Dressed in his perennial dark suit and tall hat, Cezanne carried his easel half a mile uphill to his favorite spot to rendezvous with his nemesis. Rain or shine, he lingered there for hours, mixing colors to create the perfect shade of purple. Seventeen oil paintings and twenty-four watercolors later, he had yet to find it. But he didn't give up.

But one day, he got caught in a storm and didn't make it home. Some farmers found him and carried him home, but he returned the next day.

"I want to die painting," he said.

Close enough. He died a week later.

Cezanne's muted colors, stiff shapes, and wooden-faced people never did much for me. But I bow to his struggle.

Cezanne was not a fast painter. He worked so slowly that his flowers kept wilting before he could finish painting them.

He gave up painting flowers.

People were challenging too. Sooner or later, his models couldn't help but move and lose their pose. That's why he loved the mountain. At least it stayed put.

But the sun kept moving, the light kept shifting, and the colors changed too. That may be why he couldn't conquer it. So he settled for painting vases, statues, and generously fleshed nudes with stiff faces that he modeled on wooden dolls.

He loved apples. Unlike people and flowers, apples managed to keep their position, shape, and color long enough for him to capture them on the canvas. They sit still; that's why they call them still life.

Cezanne's drab workshop in Aix-en-Provence is now a small museum. It boasts a massive northern window to steady the light, bowls of wilted apples looking like they're still waiting for him to return and immortalize their faded glow, and a curator whose enthusiasm brings Cezanne to life.

Vincent Willem Van Gogh, Provence's other eminent painter, is a whole different story.

Vincent was a clumsy Dutchman who failed at being a pastor. He decided to be a painter instead.

He struggled to paint his gloomy world, from the earthy potatoes to the farmers' humble faces and misshapen boots in murky shades of brown, beige, and gray. Then he came to Provence and exploded into a blaze of glory.

In his two years here, he painted hundreds of masterpieces bursting with color and twisted shapes pulsating with life.

Everything in Van Gogh's works throbs with energy, from people and stars to chairs and rocks.

In Provence, Van Gogh painted like a man possessed. That's why he often ran out of canvases. And, since he couldn't afford to buy more, he often painted them over or painted the new one over the old one's back. Check out New York's Met's website:

www.metmuseum.org/art/collection/search/436532

Two years and a world of difference separate the brown woman in a brown room peeling a brown potato with a gray knife on the reverse, and Van Gogh's brilliant self-portrait on the obverse. He's got a yellow hat, sharp green eyes, and an orange beard, and he inhabits an impatient universe that started swirling.

Van Gogh managed to channel Provence's maniacal intensity in his mesmerizing sunflowers, *Starry Nights*, and vibrating landscapes as he skirted the narrow edge between creativity and madness. Creativity had the lead for years, but one day, insanity won. Van Gogh cut off one of his ears and gifted it to a lady of the night, then shot himself in the wheat field he was painting.

He died three days later, but his genius never will.

Van Gogh never sold a single painting, though he gifted many. He lived from the generosity of his younger brother Theo, whose art dealer income paid for Vincent's canvases and paints, his misshaped bedroom, and his absinthe.

During his time in Saint Remy, Vincent didn't make many friends. The locals thought him strange, and they petitioned to have him locked up. He spent years in mental asylums. But today, his former cell in the Saint-Paul-de-Mausole Hospital Monastery in Saint-Rémy-de-Provence is a tiny museum and a place of holy pilgrimage for his fans, including me.

I dragged Steve there.

It's hard to believe for somebody working in the American healthcare system, where psychiatric hospitals are all but extinct, that the psychiatric hospital in Saint-Paul-de-Mausole is still active more than 150 years later. Mental health patients still shuffle up and down the worn stone stairs and roam the shady lavender gardens. And, just like their famous colleague, they paint.

Art therapy is going strong at St Paul's, where the patients' works are displayed in the cloister and sold in the museum shop alongside posters, calendars, and coffee mugs. I checked out the paintings hanging in the cloister's deep shade. They came in all styles, sizes, and colors and had little in common besides coming from Van Gogh's old asylum. But that was good enough for me.

"I want to buy one."

Steve paled. Here we are, in Europe for the foreseeable future, with no other home than the car. It may be big, but it's not a good place to hang a substantial wood-framed painting. And even I can tell that the picture won't fit in our luggage.

"I wish you wouldn't."

"But look at it! Isn't it beautiful?"

The exuberant red poppies jumped out of their frame, but Steve didn't even glance at them.

"Sure, it is. But that's not the point."

"That's exactly the point. It's beautiful, an amazing souvenir, and a fantastic conversation starter. Just imagine telling visitors that we got it at Van Gogh's asylum, and it's painted by one of his colleagues."

That did it.

The shopkeeper was clearly more used to selling mugs and posters than framed paintings. Her eyes grew big as saucers when I asked for the poppies.

"You want the frame too?"

I saw a glimmer of hope.

"Can I get it without the frame?"

"For a different price."

Ditching the frame made it 20 percent cheaper and 90 percent more manageable. Now it sits in my backpack, rolled tight and wrapped in bubble wrap, bonding with my socks.

The woman started filling out the authenticity certificate.

"Where is it going?" she asked.

I shrugged. Who knows? Wherever we go. Corsica? Malta? Italy?

"U.S. Or maybe Thailand. Does it matter?"

"Only to tell the woman who painted it. She's still here."

That rocked my world. It's October 2021, and the painting is dated 2019.

"I'm sorry."

"She's…OK. She may get out soon."

She gave me the email of the author's psychiatrist if I wanted to get in touch. I did.

Our money will go half to the author and half to the art therapy project's foundation.

"Nice," Steve said, happy with the Van Gogh T-shirt I got him with the money I'd saved from the frame.

We left Provence a few hundred dollars poorer but with our souls richer, hoping to return someday.

12

CORSICA

TIME TO MOVE ON. After being here many times, France feels like home to us. But the Mediterranean islands are new and exciting, so we decided to see them all. We'll start with Corsica, which belongs to France, then cross to Sardinia, which belongs to Italy, then head south to Sicily, which is pretty much a country in itself. Then Malta. After that, we'll cross back to the continent in Italy, where Steve swore to never drive. But that's a story for another day.

Corsica may have been part of France for the last few centuries. Still, it's not France, which became evident as soon as we boarded the ferry in Toulon. But let's let our boat-man Steve tell you about it.

The Engineer's Take: Ferry to Corsica

The first ferry trip on our tour was from mainland France to the French island of Corsica. We had a choice of several departure cities, including Marseille and Genoa. Marseille was the closest, but we chose Toulon because we expected it to be less hectic. We also had a choice of two arrival ports in Corsica, and we decided on the northernmost city of Bastia.

We booked the ferry online while we were still in the U.S.

and printed out our tickets and blank health travel declaration forms since we traveled during the Covid pandemic.

The transit takes eleven hours, and you can book en-suite cabins or reclining chairs in the main lounge. We booked a cabin because we'd had a good experience with similar accommodations on a Canadian ferry to Newfoundland a few years ago.

The instruction for the ferry included a requirement to arrive at least one hour ahead of time and an admonition to not arrive more than three hours before departure. Departure was scheduled for 8 p.m., and we arrived almost two hours earlier. We were pretty far back in the queue, so it looked like people had begun arriving at least three hours before. The ferry started boarding around seven and went very fast, with the crew yelling instructions in French and Italian — probably Corsican too.

The boarding was smooth, but the elevator up to the rooms never made it down to the parking levels, so everyone gave up and took the stairs. Since we didn't have a cabin assignment, I was worried there would be a long line at reception, but there was only one other couple ahead.

A porter unlocked the cabin to let us in, and we found a keycard on the mini desk. Like the Newfoundland ferry, the cabins were small and rudimentary, roughly 10' wide by 12' long, with a single porthole and a small bathroom and shower stall. Two single beds are bolted to the floor, and a third upper bunk can swing down over one of the beds.

Showers have high pressure and are very hot, a real pleasure after a day of traveling. The toilets are vacuum flush, just like on cruise ships.

The ferry was scheduled to arrive at 7 a.m. Around 5:30, we got an announcement that the cafeteria was open, and we had to leave the cabin by 6. We'd bought breakfast with our tickets, but it's unnecessary because you can pay as you go. And it turned out that some of the stuff I put on the tray was extra, so we had to pay some out of pocket anyhow.

It looked like at least half the people waiting in the dining room had dogs, all well-behaved, and there was at least one complaining cat. There must be a dog park somewhere on the deck where the dogs can take care of business. As a rule, dogs in France are very well-socialized and hardly ever need a leash.

Sometime after seven, they allowed us downstairs to our cars, then began the highly efficient disembarkation process involving lots of yelling in multiple languages. We drove out and started exploring Corsica's northern peninsula.

The voices of the well-built men in tight jeans and off-white wife beaters directing us inside the monster ferry's metal belly covered the noise of the cars skidding down the ramp. They didn't speak French, but their hand gestures were loud and clear. You didn't even need to hear them to understand they decried our driving ineptitude.

When Corsicans speak French, they borrow a few Italian vowels that imbue even their curses with a soft Italian melodic touch. But there's no softness or melodicity in their driving. As for the turn signals? Those are for the French.

My introduction to Corsican driving started in the tunnel letting us loose from the port. The growl of jet engines roared toward us, splitting my eardrums, and I cowered. Fortunately, they were just a couple of motorcycles that passed us like we sat still.

It got no better as we tackled the hair-raising hairpins of *Cap Corse*. That's the name of the rugged peninsula that juts north from Corsica like a raised middle finger to both France and Italy, whose edge of harsh cliffs tumbles hundreds of feet into the Mediterranean.

From an American perspective, *Cap Corse* is tiny. It's

roughly twenty miles by six, covered by forests, and home to more goats than humans. No roads dare cross its mountainous spine. Its serpentine shores are marked by black asbestos beaches, rock-carved fishing villages with crooked stone stairs for streets, and tiny vineyards that soak in the sun.

But this is not Bordeaux. Instead of Cabernet or Merlot, these grapes have strange names like *Nielluciu*, *Malvoisie*, and *Sciaccarellu*, and become wines called *Muscat* and *Impasatu*.

Once out of the tunnel, we headed north into what looked like a pleasant two-hour drive along the shore. Four hours later, we were almost halfway. We had trouble staying in our lane and stopped every few minutes to let the impatient Corsican drivers pass us by.

A lazy herd of goats sunning themselves across the road gave us a break. I tried to lure them off the road with some left-over sausage quiche, but they declined. I suspect they were vegan. I shooed them away, keeping an eye on the dignified ram whose twisted horns spelled trouble.

We stopped for lunch in the tiny fishing village of Centuri, whose eight-boat lobster fishing fleet is one of the largest in Europe.

They had *linguini alla bottarga,* one of Anthony Bourdain's favorite dishes, so, as a big fan, I couldn't resist. What a mistake! It turned out to be pasta doused in olive oil and flavored with dried grated fish roe with a rather extreme person-ality. I ate all I could take, then shared the rest with a stray Basset hound who seemed to like it way better than I did. I wonder if he ever watched *Parts Unknown*.

We cleaned our palate with some *Cap Corse* house red, nearly as forbidding as the drive, then got back to the narrow winding road teetering between the mountain and the sea. We drove by terraced gardens held up by tidy walls of flat rocks, old villages clinging to the cliff for dear life, unreally blue lagoons, and a massive abandoned asbestos factory with a million-dollar view.

By the time we made it back to Bastia, we were cooked. But the day wasn't over yet. We had yet to recover the keys to our new apartment from some local bakery, unload, and find a place to leave the car for the night. By the time Steve managed to parallel park, bullied by a hundred blowing horns and as many drivers making rude hand gestures, it had been dark for hours.

Too exhausted to go out for dinner, we shared the last of our leftover calvados and the obscure local dish I'd acquired from a nearby convenience store.

It turned out to be some animal's tongue in tomato sauce.

Oh boy. Tomorrow is another day.

13

MORE CORSICA

IT DIDN'T TAKE us long to discover that Corsica isn't America. It's not even France.

In Corsica, cows have horns, cats have claws, and dogs have balls. Here, men are men, and women are absent. The only woman in sight at a roadside café full of customers that downed their eye-openers was the waitress.

And for a tiny little island, Corsica has tons of attitude.

It starts with her kilometers. My whole life, I thought kilometers were shorter than miles. Roughly 2/3 of a mile, therefore, easier to tackle.

It turns out that Corsica didn't get that memo.

We thought that the first day, when we took a whole day to drive a hundred kilometers, was an aberration. It turns out it's the norm.

You wake up in the morning, down a couple of strong coffees, then sit with Mr. Google and negotiate a day trip of, say, 120 kilometers — that's about eighty miles. That should take about two hours, he says. You shake hands on the deal, get in the car, and drive. Ten hours later, you're almost home after cutting out the last third of the trip.

WTF?

It's the curves, of course. I call them curves to be polite and give them a sensual undertone of seduction. But ten minutes into the trip, seduction couldn't be further from my mind. I open the window and breathe in the freezing draft, longing for a puke bag.

"Watch! Watch!" Steve says, waking me up from my motion-sickness hell.

I open my eyes. There's nothing but the road.

"Watch what?" I blurt.

"There's no curve! The road's straight! You're about to miss it."

But wait, there's so much more. Narrow roads made for nimble cars, not a monster like ours. Dozens of goats chill on the road. Spectacular vistas force you to stop for pictures. Harried drivers climb up Steve's assets, causing him to pull off and let them go. And many, way too many, little monuments at the side of the road — crosses, statues, or engraved stones covered with fresh flowers, candles, and icons telling you that somebody's loved one died here.

But enough about roads. Let's talk about food.

Corsica isn't France or Italy, though it's deeply connected with both. Over its long and troubled history, Corsica has been Genoese, Pisan, and even somewhat Spanish and a little English. Now it's French, but it still has its own identity, culture, and cuisine. You'll rarely see escargots on Corsican menus. What Corsica eats is meat and lots of it.

Most menus start with *Corse plate de degustation,* a Corsican tasting platter. That's a platter with various cured, dried, and smoked meats served with crusty, chewy bread and fig jam. Occasionally, you may see a *chèvre chaud,* a warm goat cheese salad, but then the main dish is cured meat.

There's seafood, of course, and fish and pasta. But more

often, it's stuffed eggplant with ground beef, veal with olives, beef tongue with capers, or beef tripe with tomato sauce served with boiled pasta or boiled potatoes. It's a hearty, savory, unfussy cuisine bearing little resemblance to Normandy's creamy sauces or Provence's explosion of flavors.

There are none of those sissy things that melt in your mouth or the unctuous richness of sauces, making eating effortlessly delicious. None of that!

Corsican cuisine will get you working. The bread is chewy and substantial, with a sharp, thick crust that can draw blood. The muscular "veal" has lived a long and happy life grazing in the mountains. I hope she got to say goodbye to her grandchildren before that awful day that made her end up with the olives.

The cured, smoked, dry meats are delicious. They're pretty handy, too, since you can keep them for weeks without refrigeration. But you'd better avoid dropping them on your foot.

As for the quintessentially French *crème brûlée* that usually melts in your mouth, here in Corsica, it changed its ways and turned pleasantly chewy, thanks to the added chestnuts. Bottom line: You need good teeth to enjoy Corsican cuisine. Or at least dentures.

Then the wine. Whether red, white, or rosé, it's all light, transparent, and harsh. Nothing like a smooth, melodic, voluptuous Bordeaux. Steve says that the Corse wine is coarse. That may be harsh, but it's true.

But don't tell that to the locals! They're so proud of their wines that they proudly serve them everywhere and often price them above the Bordeaux. Guess what we drank?

After two nights in Bastia, Corsica's second city and the gate to its untamed north, we headed south to Ajaccio. There, it's all about their local boy, Napoleon Bonaparte, the man who put Corsica on the map.

We visited his ugly childhood house, now a museum, and learned about the great man's origins.

Napoleon was a stubborn, difficult kid without many friends. He had a challenging personality that only his mother, Letitia, could tame. That may be why his parents sent him away to school when he was only nine, trying to mold him.

But, being who he was, he didn't make friends and got bullied a lot. Was it his arrogance? His ambition? His Corsican accent? Nobody knows. Still, he made it through military school and joined the army. That's where he found his place and tore through the ranks until he became France's emperor and her greatest hero.

The unruly Corsican kid that nobody liked gave France her time of highest glory. He came close to changing the world's history, but in 1812, he went one step too far. The French Army invaded Russia, and after more than one year of incredible sacrifice, they lost the war to General Winter. That marked the beginning of the end for the French Empire.

But not the end of Napoleon's glory. His remarkable tomb in the *Dome des Invalides* in Paris is still a pilgrimage place not only for the French but for Napoleon fans everywhere. Don't miss it if you go to Paris.

Thus updated on all things Napoleon, we left Ajaccio for Bonifacio, a charming citadel-port steeped in history. We scrambled up its cobbled streets, almost too narrow for two people to pass by each other and so steep they felt like stair-cases, wondering how they managed to preserve the medieval charm and still make room for modern comforts like running water and the internet.

We inhaled the centuries-old mold on the homes' thick stone walls, with narrow windows and short doors to dark staircases. We meandered along the ramparts, lunched watching a family of eight fighting like cats — they must have been Italian — and took a boat trip to see the island from the sea. It was a lovely way to say goodbye to Corsica.

The last evening, we sat on our balcony, sipping rum imported from the French *Outre-mers* — that's what the French call their colonies — and watched the streetlights come on.

"What do you think about Corsica?" I asked.

Steve looked at me like I was nuts.

"Are you kidding? I love it!"

"Why?"

"The mountains, one side of limestone, one side granite. The geology. The geography. The history. The boats, with all those people living on them! This has been the best place of this trip."

Coming from someone who seldom forgets to complain, that was an enthusiastic endorsement.

14

SARDINIA

Sardinia, the Mediterranean's second-largest island, is just fifty minutes south of Corsica by ferry. You eat lunch in Corsica, queue for an *Ichnusa* (the national Sardinian beer) on the ferry, and land in Sardinia with hours to kill before dinner. Especially since the Sardinian dinner is more of a supper, but more on that later. You land on another rocky island, much like the one you just left, with people just like those you left: loud, animated, and speaking with their hands. Like Steve said: If you handcuffed someone here, they'd accuse you of taking away their free speech.

And speaking about Steve: Here's *The Engineer's Take*:

Ferry to Sardinia

Our second ferry was only a 50-minute passage from southern Corsica to northern Sardinia. Still, it involved crossing the national border between France and Italy. That's usually not a problem in the EU , but nothing is normal in these pandemic times.

The vehicle staging areas for the Sardinia ferry are below the high citadel in Bonifacio at the southern tip of Corsica. The ferry ticket said to arrive at least 90 minutes before the sched-

uled departure time of one p.m. We arrived two hours early to join the queue in the first staging area. After about an hour, an attendant opened a gate to the second area and signaled us in. He checked our phone to see that we had a ticket but didn't scan it.

A security person came by, looked at the ticket again, and gave a cursory review of our passports. She also glanced at our French Pass Sanitaires (the joy of Covid travels) but didn't scan them either. She had us open the rear hatch but not any of the luggage.

The ferry from Sardinia arrived after another half hour, turned 180 degrees, and backed up to the dock. A slew of lorries mixed with passenger vehicles disembarked directly from the stern. I thought they must have therefore loaded through a bow door. The ferry then sat empty for almost half an hour before they boarded us.

Turns out there is no bow door. All vehicles turn around, then back into the ferry so that they are positioned to drive straight off the stern at the destination. We were directed to turn around, then got guided backward, all the way to the ship's bow. Instructions were all shouted in some strange Italian dialect. Our car was last, backed up to what had been a bow door that was now welded closed.

We left the car, made our way up one level to an open aft deck and cafeteria area forward, ordered a couple of local Sardinian beers, and waited to depart. We finished our beers and went out on the aft deck to look at the stunning views of Corsica's limestone and granite cliffs. The passage south to Sardinia was very smooth, with only a slight roll from the east-west swells.

Disembarkment at the port in Santa Teresa di Gallura was the reverse of embarkment, except we could drive straight off and out — no reversing this time. We left the dock in heavy

*rain. The total cost for two passengers and the car was 53
euros.*

The islands may be close in many ways, but Corsica and
Sardinia are not the same.

Corsica is French, while Sardinia is Italian, as witnessed by
the scarcity of roundabouts, the abundance of horn blowing,
and, believe it or not, a tamer driving style.

While Corsica is wild, rough, and rocky, looking like it's
custom-made for goats, Sardinia belongs to her sheep. This
island has 135 sheep per square kilometer. In case you didn't
count the sheep on your square kilometers, that's even more
than the sheep-friendly nations of Great Britain and New
Zealand can report.

Sardinia has its own rocky mountains, but it also boasts
green marshes, cow-friendly meadows, wheat fields, and
sloping hills covered with orange groves and olive trees. Not to
mention palm trees, cactuses, and torrential rains that remind
me of the tropics' summer storms.

As Steve says, Corsica is where the continents butted heads.
Here, in Sardinia, they only rubbed shoulders.

If Corsica is always exciting, Sardinia can be relaxing. At
times.

Then there are the other times.

Steve got tired of hard-to-find apartments, nonexistent parking, and complicated ways to meet the owners to obtain the
keys. So he insisted on a hotel. I got him one. It advertised
parking, Wi-Fi, and a private bathroom, so I had high hopes.

The room was everything you'd expect from an inexpensive
hotel, but for the bathroom. Don't get me wrong — the bathroom was clean, spacious, and had all the accoutrements you'd
expect a bathroom to have, and some you wouldn't, like the

bidet. If you don't know, a bidet is a fixture looking like a toilet that works like a sink — for your nether parts. I'm gonna stop here since the art of the bidet is something I have yet to master. So, the bathroom was fine, except for being four doors down the hallway.

I'd told Steve I'd booked "a room with a private external bathroom." I didn't know what that meant, but how bad could it be? As long as it doesn't rain inside, it should be all right, I thought. Even if it was an outhouse. It may involve a walk, but so what? After all that driving, we need some exercise. Plus, what can you expect for 55 euros a night?

A lot more, apparently. Steve went ballistic.

"You expect me to walk down the hallway in my underwear in the middle of the night?"

I gently pointed out that he could get dressed first, but that didn't help. His eyes popped out like a snail's, and he turned a warm shade of purple that clashed with his tan jacket. Worried that he might have a stroke, I gathered our belongings, and we returned to the reception.

The receptionist, a slight, harried woman speaking at least four languages — she'd tried them all on us — struggled to hear us above the screams of her toddler. For ten euros more, she found us a room with a bathroom. Crisis averted, I thought. I grabbed the key and the TV remote she offered me — don't ask me why — and went to find the room.

It had a bed, an en-suite bathroom, and even a TV for the remote, but no power. Therefore, no light, no TV, and no heat. We went back.

The poor woman struggled to feed her toddler, and she paled when she saw us back.

She'll send the director to check, she said. Wow, I thought. I'd send the electrician, but what do I know? Five minutes later, the lights were on, as promised. I guess the director wasn't the director for nothing.

By five, we had finally settled. Time to go out for dinner. Little did we know…

Italian restaurants, cafés, and pizzerias have a crystal-clear sense of their mission: to provide hungry people with lunch and dinner. That's why they open from noon to two, then again after seven. Because who'd ever want to eat before seven?

We walked miles and miles (kilometers, I mean) in the rain, looking for a pizzeria. We found none. Everything was closed. We were about to lose hope when we saw a man fussing around a pizza oven.

"Pizza?" I asked hopefully.

"*Si,*" he agreed. "*A dieci-nove.*" At seven.

"At seven? But it's not even six! But why? *Porche?*"

"*Solo dopo aver acceso il fuoco a legna nel forno…*" I first have to light the wood-fired oven…"

Of course. No self-respecting Sardinian would ever eat anything less than a wood-fired pizza. That takes skill, time, and patience.

But we'd run out. Soaked, frozen, and exhausted, we shuffled to our en-suite hotel room. We trudged in, dripping all over the floors. We ignored the half-dozen *carabinieri* with pistols on their hip, watching Sponge Bob with the toddler. We drank our own wine and ate some of the eternal Corsican sausages we lug around for times like this.

"I don't like Sardinia," Steve said, glaring at the TV with no English channels.

We'd been there for almost three hours.

"Why don't you wait until tomorrow to decide?"

He shook his head and went to sleep.

I woke up at three, as usual, and got working on my books.

I'd been up for hours when they began hammering pipes at six-thirty.

It's got to be an emergency, I thought. But the banging returned at 6:40, 6:52, and 7. Boy, they've got bad pipes here, I thought. Then we went for breakfast, and I discovered the hammering noise was just the barista cleaning the espresso machine by slamming the basket against the sink.

This is not like home.

But if we wanted it to be like home, we should have stayed there. These people aren't about to change their ways to please us. So, to function, we'll have to adapt. When in Sardinia… we'll do like Sardinians do. We'll adopt the siesta, the late dinner, and everything else, and we'll live like they do. We'll try, at least.

BTW, did you know that the word "sardonic" comes from Sardinia? Today we ran on fumes. We tried three gas stations but couldn't get gas because the machine didn't accept my credit card PIN. Then we got stuck in Tempo Pausania's historic center. The streets were so narrow that Steve folded the mirrors, but that still wasn't enough. We ended up blocking the traffic until three *carabinieri* redirected it and came to help us out. Steve backed up like a pro, with less than two inches between the car and the thousand-years-old stone walls.

We thanked them profusely. They waved us off and laughed, and I finally got it. Sardonic it is.

15

A RANDOM BUNCH OF SARDINIAN ODDITIES

1. Coral

Alghero, Sardinia's old port, turns out to be the world's coral capital. Who knew? First, that coral even had a capital. And second, that it's here.

Alghero's tiny coral museum taught us more about coral than I ever needed to know. It also delighted us with the extraordinary coral artworks by local artisans who still practice the craft. Sardinians have been harvesting Mediterranean red coral since Nuragic times — that's prehistory, roughly 3,000 years ago. They kept doing it through Roman times, then the Middle Ages. Not long ago, they noticed they were running out of coral.

They moved to responsible, sustainable harvesting. These days they only distribute twenty-five coral harvesting permits a year, all time and space limited. No coral gets collected unless it's at least fifty meters deep. They also started an impressive campaign to rebuild the coral marine life. In case you don't know much about coral, like me, here's a primer:

a. Coral is not a plant. It's an animal.

b. Not really. It's many, many animals living together in a colony.

c. They share a digestive system. The food — plankton, crustacean parts, cold pizza, or whatever happens to be on the menu, gets swallowed by one coral to eventually get pooped by the last. Talk about sharing!

d. They reproduce sexually by sperm. The males release it in the water, and it magically finds its way to the females to generate the young ones. Go figure! And for years, whenever someone said they got pregnant from swimming in a communal pool, I thought it was nonsense!

e. They also reproduce asexually. When broken pieces of a colony find a good spot, they settle and grow roots. Seeing d., that sounds like an excellent idea.

f. Scientists are regenerating dying colonies by introducing new ones. And they're pretty successful, but for the excruciatingly slow coral growth rate. Some take a hundred years to grow a couple of feet tall. Imagine if that happened to your kids!

g. The part used for jewelry is their orange-red skeleton made of calcium carbonate.

h. That's it. By now, you know more about coral than you need to. Except that it's beautiful.

2. Cork

Cork is another Sardinian staple. If you didn't know, cork is the bark of cork trees, a species of oak. Planting cork trees is the ultimate example of selflessness since they take up to forty years to deliver their first harvest. After that, they provide another crop every nine years. Those who plant them clearly do it for their grandkids.

Cork trees may get stripped sixteen times or so in their two hundred years. And it's not pretty. After harvesting, the naked trunks stand smooth, red, and vulnerable, hiding under their green crown of leaves like a forest of skinless bodies. It hurts to watch.

Still, cork has a lot of benefits. It makes wine stoppers, floor tiles, bags, belts, wallets, and just about anything you can imagine. Plus, the cork trees absorb massive amounts of CO_2, especially after being skinned. Harvesting increases their CO_2 uptake by three to five times.

3. Rocks

There's no shortage of rocks in Sardinia. Most fields are covered in scattered rocks the size of watermelons, remnants from glacier melt. And they're a nuisance, making it hard to work the fields. That's why the locals gather them into tall piles or build them into elaborate walls to clear the fields for the artichokes, vines, and cork crops. Same with the green pastures covered in herds of wet sheep whose stick feet buckle under the weight.

4. Writers

Oddly enough for such a patriarchal land, Sardinia's most famous writer was a woman. Grazia Delleda received her Nobel prize in 1926 and spoke the shortest "thank you" speech the old white male club academy had ever heard.

Grazia was born in Nuoro. Her childhood home is now a small museum featuring her grandma's pantry, loaded with potatoes, garlic, and slabs of smoked pork fat. It's also home to her many unsmiling pictures.

That girl wouldn't smile to save her life. I wonder if she had rotten teeth. Even when she almost broke into a smile upon receiving her Nobel prize, she caught herself just in time and hid her mouth in her fur collar.

But, bad teeth or not, she wrote passionately about the Sardinia she loved.

"We are Sardinians.

We are Spaniards, Africans, Phoenicians, Carthaginians, Romans, Arabs, Pisani, Byzantines, Piedmontese.

We are the golden-yellow broom that showers onto rocky trails like huge lamps ablaze.

We are the wild solitude, the immense and profound silence, the brilliance of the sky, the white flower of the cistus.

We are the uninterrupted reign of the mastic tree, of the waves that stream over ancient granite, of the dog-rose, of the wind, of the immensity of the sea.

We are a land of long silences, of horizons vast and pure, of plants glum, of mountains burnt by the sun and vengeance.

We are Sardinians."

Translation ©Matilda Colarossi 2019

5. Bandits.

The Sardinian flag features four dark bandits' heads on a white field divided by red stripes. That's a nod to Sardinia's history of banditry, now presumably over. Maybe. The same image flies on the boats and graces the label of *Inchusa*, and all Sardinian things that matter. As a side note, the Corsican flag has a similar bandit, but he's alone.

The former bandit's lair, Orgosolo, perched in the heart of the Sardinian mountains, is newly famous for its street art.

To keep his hot-headed students out of trouble, a high-school teacher got them to paint the city walls. A few years and two hundred paintings later, tourists come to see Orgosolo for its famous graffiti, which are more than street art — they're a political message.

The unsmiling locals' suspicious faces lit up when they saw us chasing the murals. They even took us to show us the best ones and struggled to explain what they meant. We smiled, nodded, and agreed, hoping they weren't asking for our wallets. But we tried to foster friendship and cooperation.

We crisscrossed Sardinia every which way, and I can tell you there's no end to her quirks. Like the noise. Sardinians are indeed loud for a nation that mostly speaks with their hands! They start early in the morning and keep screaming, banging, hammering, and rebuilding their engines until bedtime.

Then the smells. The back streets here don't smell good. This isn't France, where public toilets grace every corner and water trucks wash the streets every morning. Here, all smells, from beer to cats, are authentic and pungent.

Even the flamingos are different. They bend their defective knees backward, like everywhere else, but refuse to be pink. They're black and white, likely because of their diet. All flamingos come out white and turn pink a year later because of the pink carotene in the shrimp they eat. But apparently, Sardinian shrimp didn't get the memo, so Sardinian flamingos are stuck looking like a bunch of crooked-nosed pathetic storks instead of being pink.

Much like Corsica, Sardinia feels way bigger than it looks on the map. It's just one of Italy's islands and not the biggest one at that, but it feels like a country. Its kilometers are longer than most miles, so it took us a while to explore its countless beaches, mountains, cities, and lovely fields and marshes. There's no end to the things to discover.

"It's a hidden gem," Steve says.

I have to agree.

16

EATING AND DRINKING IN SARDINIA

IF YOU THINK the French are obsessed with their food, wait until you get to Italy. It may be too early to tell since Sardinia is our first Italian stop, but I'd be surprised if the trend didn't continue.

Italian breakfasts are no big deal — usually just a thimble of espresso or a cappuccino, and a pastry that you inhale leaning over the counter since it's cheaper than sitting at the table. But lunches are serious business.

We found that out over dinner, as we delighted in mouth-watering pizzas at the pizzeria down the road. I had the "raw" pizza — a heavenly light, thin crust adorned with prosciutto, arugula, and a layer of melty Mozzarella so stretchy I could wrap myself in it. Steve ordered a *pizza quattro stagioni* — four seasons.

That's the kind of pizza you order when you can't get your friends to agree with you. You want pepperoni — they don't. You love anchovies — they'd rather have olives — and so on. It's like four pizzas in one, every one different, so you can share, but you still get what you like.

Not here. Alghero's *quatro stagioni* must have been affected by global warming. It had everything everywhere, just like the strange weather we'd been having. To be fair, pizzas here may be as large as a truck tire, but they're individual, so there's no need to divide them, but still.

Steve was still struggling to separate his olives from his ham when I asked the lovely Sardinian server:

"Are you open for lunch?"

She shook her head.

"No, sorry. We're just a pizzeria. We only open for dinner."

That was a shocker. If pizza isn't lunch food, then what is?

"People here don't have pizza for lunch?"

"No. Lunch is our big meal."

She was right, as we discovered the next day. It happened to be Sunday, and, as always, between half the places being closed for church and everyone eating out, we were lucky to find a table in a traditional restaurant downtown.

The place was hopping. The dozen small square tables were packed with people chatting, laughing, and speaking with their hands without spilling their wine. They must have had lots of practice. The wine list was not a list. It was a massive cupboard full of wines; you just pointed to the one you wanted. The ancient desk bar was decorated with mini bottles of liquors and aperitifs and a few black-and-white photos. The one in the middle looked familiar.

"I know that guy! Is that Picasso or Toscanini?"

Steve shrugged.

"Why would they have Picasso here? He wasn't even Italian. He was Spanish. And French."

He was right, of course. But those haunted eyes... the deep wrinkles... the shiny scalp..., the intense gaze...

I asked the waiter.

"Who's that?"

He glanced in that direction.

"*La madre del directore*," he said, pouring wine. "The owner's mother."

I shook my head.

"No, not the lady in the middle. The one on top. The old man with haunting eyes."

"*Si, si. C'esta la sua mamma*. Yes. That's his mother."

Steve choked on his wine. I smiled, nodded, and kicked him under the table. Do I have a way with words or what?

Either way, we spent a few good hours enjoying the *antipasti* — appetizers — then the *primi* — a choice of pasta or risotto — then the *secondi* — *di mare* or *di terra*. We skipped dessert, coffee, and the digestive. We also skipped dinner.

How can these people eat like that every day and not get fat? Beats me.

Sardinian food is divided between the catch of the sea and the fruit of the land. Every Sardinian menu I've seen had a menu *di mare,* with *primi* and *secondi*, and one *di terra*. Sometimes that goes for the *antipasti* too. Not for the dessert. Yet.

They seem to share a sincere — and inexplicable to me — affection for *bottarga*. *Bottarga* is dried fish roe. They love to put it in pasta, salads, and just about everything else. They'd put it in the dessert, too, if you let them. They'll happily explain what kind of fish it came from like it matters. All I know is that it's fishy. Seriously fishy. My first *bottarga* scarred me for life. Ever since that, I've avoided it like the plague. But I didn't go hungry. They have plenty more oddities, and most are delicious.

Sardinian pastas are not long, slim, and tedious, like our ubiquitous spaghetti and linguini. They have exotic names like *lorighittas*, shaped like the rings used to tie horses, and *laditas*, made with lard. *Andarinos*, which get dried in the sun; *maloreddus*, which look like seashells; and *fregola*, which look like lentils and get toasted in the oven. Their unusual tastes and strange organic shapes make you think of yet-undiscovered life forms. They swim in fishy sauces like the ever-present *bottarga* or *ricci* (sea urchin) or get served with all sorts of sea creatures like *cozze* (clams), tiny octopi no bigger than my pinky nail, or tender calamari and minuscule pink shrimps that you eat with their shell.

There's *maharrones ala moda nostra*, little artisanal pasta looking like mealworms served with a sauce of squash and shrimp; and *polpo*, deliciously grilled crispy octopus. Or *culurgioni*, also known as *agnolotti*, little pillowy things filled with pecorino and mint bathed in an orange-flavored sauce in the north and tomato and sausage in the south.

The *secondi* — what we'd call the main dish — are often mixed seafood, fried or grilled, or fillets of unique fish you won't find anywhere else. Unless it's *polpo* — pink tender octopus bathed in pesto. The *secondi di terra* may be *braciolla di maiale*, pork chop; *vitello*, a chunk of slow-cooked beef still chewy after marinating in wine and cooking for hours; or, more likely, *cavallo,* horse steak, cooked rare, with meat so lean and clean it's almost flavorless. And they all come on their own.

Unlike America, where everything comes with sides, and often salads, here, if you want sides, you order them. And pay. A medium-sized serving of fries will set you back five euros; a side of rice or veggies will be slightly less. This is Keto heaven — you may get bread, but not much. And the butter? What butter?

Desserts are traditional: *sede*, a large flat *raviolo* filled with ricotta, fried, and drizzled with honey; *tiramisu*; or sometimes, *crème brûlée*.

Another surprise was *focaccia*. Unlike American focaccia, which is just undercooked greasy flatbread with a smattering of sliced tomatoes, Sardinian *focaccia* is a delicious sandwich of fresh crispy bread baked in a square loaf as big as China, cut into diamonds and filled with deliciousness.

Sardinian wines aren't quite Bordeaux, but they'd beat the Corse wines any day of the week with both hands tied behind their back. The local red, the *Cannoneau*, is a bit thin and rough, but it's still a cut above the Corsicans. But the *Bovia*? The *Rocca Rubria Carrigano*? Now you're talking! Their energy and vigor fill your mouth with the smooth, sensual flavor of ripe dark fruit and enough strong tannins to tame the wildest *bottarga*.

The whites aren't bad either, especially the *Vermentino*. They're cool and light with smooth, fruity notes reminiscent of *Sauvignon Blanc*.

All in all, be assured that you won't go hungry.

17

SARDINIAN HOMES

Most Sardinian homes seem to be apartments. They're small, functional, and attractive, with locks that would make a prison proud — the one I'm looking at right now has five deadbolts. They have narrow windows that keep out the light and thick cold walls that suck in your body heat. We've had our heater set at max for the last two days, but I'm still wearing my down hoodie, though not the hood. Truth be told, it's winter, to which the locals resign themselves like it's a mandatory evil. They just shiver and grab an extra blanket. Their homes are built to keep out Mediterranean summers' unrelenting heat and harsh sun, not to keep them warm in winter.

Most furniture comes from IKEA. It does its job, but the sofas don't invite you to linger. Which is good since we're not here to linger. We're here to explore.

Most TVs only speak Italian, except the one in Nuoro, which had a French channel speaking only English. Everything else is Italian only: the news, soccer, *Dancing with the Stars*, the *Food Channel*, and John Wayne's dubbed old westerns.

Clocks are everywhere, and they're all stopped. This one in the kitchen is the size of a family pizza. It's set at ten to eight, like all the others. For days now, I've wondered why. Did something happen at ten to eight that froze all Sardinian clocks for eternity? And is it ten to eight in the morning or the evening? And why ten to eight? Let me know if you figure it out.

Sardinian bathrooms are weird. They're large — enormous even, compared to the size of the homes. You're lucky if you have room to get off the bed instead of crawling over each other. But the bathrooms are massive. They have sinks, showers, and toilets, of course, and they all have a bidet.

A bidet is a porcelain bowl. It looks like a toilet, but for the lack of cover and the tap spraying a water jet meant to clean your privates.

Don't get me wrong, now. I'm all for clean privates; I have no doubt they improve one's quality of life, but spending valuable square meters you don't have for that purpose alone? Isn't that weird? Kind of like having a special place to brush your teeth that's different from where you wash your hands. I'd love to ask someone about this, but I haven't yet gotten that intimate with any of the natives to inquire how they clean their privates, so I'm struggling to figure it out on my own.

They even have special detergents for this purpose. Not soap, not shampoo, not shower gel. They have something called *Detergente Intimo Ultradelicato,* "Very Delicate Intimate Detergent," that "respects the areas subject to dryness and irritation and is so bio-active that hydrates, with probiotics, prebiotics, hyaluronic acid, tea tree, grapefruit, and sage extract."

That's fascinating, especially considering that half the homes have no ovens or washing machines, few have dishwashers, and I'm still waiting to meet a dryer.

And I bet there's some old superstition saying you get cursed with the *mallochio*, the evil eye, should the bathroom be on the same level as the bedroom. There's always at least one step lying in wait to trip you in the dark as you fumble half-asleep without knowing if you're heading to the bathroom or the closet. And, since we're always on the move, we never remember what's where. Between that and the ropes Steve stretched across the room for the laundry, every step is a life-threatening adventure.

Finally, recycling. To take out the trash in Sardinia, you need a PhD.

They have five separate color-coded containers that go out on different days of the week.

- One for humid organics, like food
- One for plastic
- One for paper and cardboard
- One for undifferentiated dry products — whatever that means
- One for glass and aluminum

I tried and tried, but I still find that baffling, and I usually get it wrong. You try it:

Do greasy pizza boxes go with the humid organics or the cardboard?

How about the used floss? Dirty yogurt containers? Aluminum-plated cardboard? Human nails?

You could put them with the humid organics if you wet them first, I guess. How about used Q-tips?

Plus, all the trash containers in the street are LOCKED!

Of course. You wouldn't want anyone stealing your garbage. Not after working so hard to sort it!

18

THE THINGS WE CARRY

THIS NEW LIFESTYLE of moving from one stranger's home to another every other day teaches you to be self-reliant. If there's something you can't live without, you'd better carry it with you. These are some of mine:

1. Instant coffee. Most places have some sort of coffee maker or another, but some don't. Even when they do, having a coffeemaker doesn't mean you have coffee. And the variety of coffee makers, from the newest Nespresso machines to the kind your grandmother used to set on the fire, would make my head spin on a good day. But for me, no day is a good day before I have my coffee. Figuring out how to unscrew the thing to fill it with water and plant in the coffee is too much for my muddled morning brain. Before I have my coffee, I can't even figure out which button to push, so instant coffee it is until Steve wakes up to make us coffee. But by that time, I'm usually buzzing big-time after two or three stiff mugs.

2. Toilet paper. Even the best-equipped places forget to leave that extra roll of toilet paper, and there are few things more desperately needed when you're all alone. That's why we

always have some with us — ever since we ran out in Paris and had to go Eastern style.

3. Motrin and Tylenol. I always have some on hand since a few years ago when I ran out of Motrin in Japan. I spent a few exciting minutes pantomiming "migraine" to an enthralled audience of Japanese pharmacists. I'm just glad it wasn't diarrhea.

4. Alcohol. There's nothing like a sip of liquor to warm up weary bones and take off the edge after long, trying days. You're exhausted after folding your mirrors to navigate the narrow streets, spending your last bit of energy on finding a place to park, and running on fumes to find your home for the night. It's late, cold, and dark, and you don't even know where to go. That's when a glass of wine works wonders. BTW, glasses come in handy, too, especially for picnics.

5. Something to eat. See above. I always carry bread, cheese, and smoked meats that don't need refrigeration — thank you, Corsica. Dark chocolate. Also, fruit, peppers, lemons, and whatever leftovers we happen to own. Pizza, especially. After working in the ER for years, cold pizza is like mother's milk to me.

6. Laundry detergent. Once in a great while, you happen upon a washing machine, and you want to make the most of it since clean clothes make everything feel better. But if washing machines are rare, laundry detergent is even rarer. That's why I carry pods. They're easy to pack and easy to use.

7. Pepper. We were in Buenos Aires the first time the lack of pepper threw me into an existential crisis. Those Argentines have handsome gauchos and sizzling steaks bigger than your plate. The meat is plentiful, and so's the lovely wine that goes with it. And they have salt, but pepper? Not so much. I asked for it, but the Argentinian waiters looked at me in wonder. They couldn't understand what I needed it for. So I took it as a fact of life:

Argentina has no pepper. But Italy? Whenever I ask for crushed red pepper for my pizza, I'm lucky if they give me a little paper packet of black pepper. The one time they brought some cayenne, I stole it. So I bought a pepper mill that I carry in my pocket.

8. Rope. That's Steve's domain. He knows knots since he used to sail. It turns out that washing your clothes is good, but it's seldom enough. They usually need drying, too, though there was a time or two I ended up putting on my newly washed underwear. Talk about freshness! But I digress. If washing machines are rare in Sardinia, dryers are practically unheard of. That's when Steve saves the day. He stretches his parachute cord as high as the low ceilings permit, but he still risks a strangulation injury. Thankfully, I'm short enough to only have the wet clothes caressing my head.

9. Corkscrew and knife. Few things in life are more frustrating than having a bottle of good wine you can't open. Beating it with your shoe? Heating the neck to get the cork out? That's poppycock. Some of the best things in life require a corkscrew. Or a bit of luck. The other day we felt adventurous and took a turn through an abandoned mine. We ended up in *Spiagia di Piscinas*, a lovely beach that boasts the tallest sand dunes in the Mediterranean. An excellent place to picnic, I thought. So I laid my raincoat over the hood and dug into our supplies. We were halfway through the dried sausage when a car full of Romanians stopped by, looking forlorn. It turns out they had wine but no corkscrew. "Would you happen to have a corkscrew?" one of them asked me in French. I frowned. "What kind of Romanians are you, without a corkscrew?" I questioned. He apologized profusely. "I'm sorry, we flew with only the hand luggage, so we couldn't bring one!"

"You should have bought one when you bought the wine," I lectured, then lent them my Opinel, the knife/corkscrew some friends gifted us before we left. It's a killer! The corkscrew is nice, but that knife is for real! You could hunt boar with it if you could find them.

10. Crocs. You wouldn't think crocs are worth carrying when you try to travel light, but you'd be wrong. The more you travel, the more your feet need rest, and your shoes need to breathe. I don't walk barefoot in strangers' homes, so two months into our trip, my Crocs have been worth their weight in gold (they're really light).

11. Plug adapters and chargers because if having an iPhone is nice, having one that works is even nicer.

12. Zipper bags of all sizes for all the oddities you collect along the way, from seashells to the bread stolen from the breakfast buffet.

19

CEFALU

Moving on. After a lovely week in Sardinia, we left for Sicily. That was another overnight ferry ride, but by now, we were pros.

It was still dark at 5:30 when the crackly loudspeakers woke us up on the ferry to Palermo. We headed to the fifth-deck bar for a very Italian breakfast: your choice of croissant, served on a napkin, and your choice of coffee, served in a paper cup. We sipped our coffees, watching sleepy travelers shuffle in with their bags/kids/dogs/backpacks/potties. Leaving the ferry was a breeze, but for Gwendolyn, our navigator, insisting that Cefalu, our home for the day, supposed to be an hour away, was 400 kilometers further. Sharp as usual, Gwendolyn hadn't figured out we'd left Sardinia.

As we left the dock to enter Palermo, the first thing that struck us was the garbage. It flew through the streets; it covered the sidewalks; it hung from the fences. There was nothing but trash everywhere you looked, so we wondered if the sanitation workers were on strike. That's one thing with Italy — you never know who's on strike: train workers, bus drivers, sanitation workers. The one thing you know is that it's going to hurt you.

Still, not our problem. Not yet. So we rushed out of Palermo like all the other cars.

That's how we learned lesson #2: Driving in Sicily is a negotiation.

Like everywhere else, they have traffic lights, crosswalks, and priority signs. But here, they're suggestions rather than recommendations, let alone rules. Like when we got to a roundabout behind a man pushing a heavy cart through it. He signaled us to pass him, ignoring the incoming motorcycle. Or the countless times we had the green light to turn left, but everyone else got in our way.

Driving in Sicily is an adventure. Fortunately, we didn't have far to go since Cefalu, the sleepy fishing village I had booked us in for the night, was close.

We found our villa, parked the car, and then took a long walk along the shore to look for a bathroom. But, since this is no longer France but Italy, the bathrooms are few and far between. Just as we were getting desperate, we found a coffee shop. Three euros bought us bathroom privileges, plus a cappuccino and a mouthwatering pistachio triangle. Not to mention a chance to eye the locals.

At most restaurants in Italy, prices depend on your standing. Not in society, but in the café. Sitting at the table is more expensive, so if you want to save, you munch your croissant and down your espresso leaning against the counter, greeting the newcomers, and checking out the waitress's endowments.

We partook of the bathrooms and watched the locals flirt with the waitress and shout at each other across the room, gesticulating wildly without spilling their coffee. It's a skill I envy. I can spill my drink just by looking at it, preferably over my laptop. That's how I keep Apple in business. But I digress.

We left the café and stumbled along the ankle-breaking cobbled streets to the majestic thousand-year-old Cefalu cathedral. It was built in the eleventh century by Roger the Second, the Norman King of Sardinia. He hoped to gain fame and unify the country. It worked, even though he didn't live to see it.

The Norman-style cathedral is built like a fortress. The thick stone walls are seldom broken by narrow slanted windows meant for archers. Up above, the sturdy crenelated towers are watchtowers rather than church towers, so they built another tower next door for the church bell.

But the miracle of faith lives on inside. Christ Pantocrator's (Almighty's) thousand-year-old gilded mosaic keeps a keen eye on tourists and faithful alike and thumbs its long Byzantine nose at the disgraceful stained-glass windows commissioned in 2003. I found them beautiful, but their abstract art scandalized the town. Where are the saints? Virgin Mary? How about the cross?

They do have a point. I squinted, trying to make up the last judgment in the abstract rose window above the door, but I saw nothing but a dazzling array of colors.

We left the cathedral to scramble up more steep streets. We dodged growling scooters and chased haughty cats looking for the hike to La Rocca, a ruined Norman castle 800 feet above. We finally found it, but the gate was locked. "Closed due to inclement weather."

We stared at the perfectly cloudless blue sky; we looked at each other, shrugged, and went to get lunch.

Along the way, we happened upon Cefalu's famous medieval laundry. It's a lovely cave carved inside the city wall where the village women came to do their laundry and gossip until not long ago. They rubbed the dirty clothes against the rough slanted stones, rinsed them in the clean spring water that flushed the dirt into the sea, and watched their children play while catching up on the news. No wonder this place was Cefalu's heart for centuries.

Nearby, we found an open restaurant built inside the city wall, just like the neighboring houses. It had an incredible view over the Mediterranean but not enough room for the two over-sized American strollers parked between the tables. But we managed to crawl to a table with a view and ordered our first Sicilian lunch.

Steve's *primo* was the special *Spaghetti al Nero di Seppia*, pasta with squid ink, which he found bafflingly black. I tried the *zuppa de cozze* — mussels soup, which was mostly *cozze* and not much soup. Steve's secondo, the *vitello alla marsala*, had clearly enjoyed a long and active life, just like every other veal we encountered in Italy. It took some work, but it was tasty. As for my *involtino,*(stuffed meat roll,)… let's talk wine instead. The house wine, a *Nero D'Avola*, started harsh but grew smoother with each sip. We ended with *cannoli* — how could we not? There's nothing more Sicilian than *cannoli*, not even the Mafia.

Thus full of food and wine, we shuffled to our villa, ready to take on Sicily.

20

LIVING IN OTHER PEOPLE'S HOMES

THERE'S something seriously weird about living in other people's homes. We've never done it — in fact, I like my privacy so much that I even avoid staying with friends and family. But the hosting rooms' landscape has changed so dramatically over the last few years that you don't really have a choice.

Booking.com and Hotels.com used to be 98 percent hotels, with a rare managed apartment thrown in for good measure. But these days, if you sort them by ranking — which I do — and by price — which I also do — 95 percent of the best-looking places are privately owned, whether they're B&Bs, apartments, or just odd rooms in people's homes.

Add to that VRBO and Home Exchange, and you'll find yourself living in some stranger's home, drying yourself with their towels, sleeping on their pillows, and peeping in their sock drawers.

That's half creepy and half mesmerizing, especially when it happens to be someone's actual house, like the apartment in Aix-en-Provence. Compound the voyeurism with the ongoing sense of adventure since you never know how things work, from the induction stove to the recycling, and you find yourself in seriously kinky territory.

Take the place in Aix-en-Provence that I told you about. It was modest, functional, and exceptionally well-designed. And diagnostic of its owners. It had a wire pulling the garbage pail open as you opened the trash door. Also, drawers within drawers that sheltered the most impressive spice collection I've ever seen — and I'm a connoisseur since I collect spices like others collect stamps. There was a tome of instructions on everything from how to make coffee and how to dry the dishes to where to buy the best croissants. You could tell this was the home of a childless, petless mature couple with a settled life and an impressive dose of OCD.

I resisted opening any closets and drawers I had no business in. But I couldn't overlook the books — a whole shelf on travel, another on linguistics, and one shelf bending under the weight of atlases and encyclopedias. I marveled at the ultra-modern art, the many '80s CDs, and the breathtaking array of "*bio*" products, from the compostable coffee pods to the vegan sea salt (as opposed to the animal ones?) and the bio-detergents (they suck). Oh, how I longed for my good old Windex!

Inhabiting someone's home forces you to learn about them. That holds true even for the cheap rentals with no closets, thin towels, deformed cutlery, and mismatched glasses.

But, more than anything, you learn to adapt. You discover that the things you thought you couldn't live without, like microwaves, toilet paper holders near the toilet seat, fast internet, toasters, switches you flip down to turn off, knobs on the outside of doors, and news in English, are all optional. Sometimes they're there, more often not. Every new home teaches you something.

As we moved about every other day, every new place we stayed at challenged our assumptions and caused us hours of consternation. In Bayeux, we managed to lock the induction stove, so we couldn't use it for two days. The hot water seemed to come from somewhere else, in circumstances we weren't privy to, so we never got a shower.

In Paris, I had to run the laundry three times through the machine before I got it to spin so we could hang it to dry. The dehumidifier in Dinan kept us awake at night and needed emptying every morning. The Alghero coffee maker was an antique. You set it on the stove and boil it until all the water evaporates through the coffee layer to make coffee. That one I never mastered, so I had to wait for Steve to wake up. The Cagliari apartment had a color-coded garbage sorting chart for each day of the week and five separate trash containers. It took us hours to find the Wi-Fi password on the wall side of the repeater in Palermo and three days to accept that the air conditioners really didn't give heat.

Wherever you go, you're in for a surprise. You need to be nimble and willing to adapt; otherwise, every stay would be a disaster.

Some are anyhow, like that place in Nuoro that we couldn't reach by car. It took us hours to acquire enough coins to park downtown. We then dragged our luggage to the apartment only to discover that two sets of stairs separated the bedroom from the bathroom, and the internet didn't work. We cursed, carried our bags back to the car, and found somewhere else to stay.

Every place you inhabit teaches you about the people, the country, and yourself. Every abode we survived built our skills and confidence. It took me a while, but I'm proud to say that I can toast bread in a frying pan and reheat food without a microwave or an oven — without burning it to ashes.

21

A SICILIAN THANKSGIVING

IT FEELS like a lifetime since we left Paris, but it's not. It's just the last week in November, and Thanksgiving is looming.

Steve and I are no strangers to odd holidays. For us, they're pretty much the norm. This is what I wrote last year:

"Christmas Day found Steve, Guinness, and me on the edge of Lake Thurmond in Georgia. We're socially isolating in our 22-foot RV, braving the subfreezing weather, and facing the challenge of another strange Christmas dinner.

"Strange Christmas dinners are our thing. I remember London twenty years ago when nothing was open on Christmas, not even the metro. Luckily, we found a convenience store where a tired lady in a burqa sold us tahini, falafel, hummus, and yogurt. We feasted on a white towel spread over the sofa in the Waterloo Holiday Inn.

"Then that time in Virginia when everything was closed but the Chinese restaurant. We had General Tao's chicken with fried rice for Christmas dinner and opened our own wine with a knife since they didn't have a corkscrew.

"Then that time on a sailboat in the British Virgin Islands. I bought a goose too big for the oven, so Steve had to trim it.

Unbeknownst to me, he got rid of the trimmings by throwing them out the porthole as I sat outside to watch the kids swim. They were having a blast when the water around the boat suddenly started boiling. I wondered why until I saw that it was thick with barracudas who had come to enjoy Christmas dinner. Up to this day, I'm not sure if they were after the goose or the kids, but I managed to get them out intact. But at least it was warm.

"Not now. We sit behind the RV to shelter from the wind and shiver, though we're wrapped in every article of clothing we own and sip on Bourbon from coffee mugs since the campground forbids alcohol. We watch the blizzard shake the neighbors' Christmas decorations and listen to remote Christmas carols as we wait for the buns to unfreeze so I can stuff them with the two-day-old pulled pork. (I'm talking about the bread, you all.)."

That was last year. Now we're in Sicily.

We drove from Cefalu to Palermo and started scouring the streets to look for my booked apartment. Steve braved the narrow roads clogged with construction trucks, battered cars, growling scooters, and the occasional tired horse but couldn't get us there. Surprise, surprise — the place was in the "ZTL," the reserved area closed to all but local traffic. That's common in Italy, to curb the traffic in the centuries-old city centers.

There was no way in. So Steve dropped me off and drove away, looking for a place to park. I stumbled under the combined weight of our two computers, iPads, food, and dirty laundry, looking for our new home. I didn't have much fun, but the local kids loved it. They must have thought I was an early Santa, and they started following me.

By the time they started getting cheeky, I'd found our temporary home on the second floor of a dilapidated building inside one of Palermo's oldest markets. I handed a sweaty gentleman named Felipe thirty euros for the cleaning, he gave me the keys, and voilà: I was home, minus Steve, the car, the phone, and the internet, which was sadly missing.

By the time Steve managed to get rid of the car and find the apartment, we were both too exhausted to look for turkeys. We gave in to the warm invite of the aproned gentleman across the street. With a dazzling smile and lots of hand motions, he invited us into his little restaurant that advertised good food for less.

The half-dozen flushed revelers inside welcomed us with open arms. We smiled, nodded, and sat at a plastic table by the kitchen. I found the menu on a board on the wall and started reading it to Steve, but it turned out to be premature.

The smiling owner returned.

"Vino?" Wine? I asked, hoping for a list.

He smiled and nodded.

"*Bianco o rosso?* White or red?"

"Red," I said.

"Water?"

"Yes."

"*Naturale o frizzante*?" Still or sparkling?

"Sparkling."

He went to get glasses and chat with the tired-looking woman who manned the stove.

I studied the board. It featured two *antipasti,* a few *primi,* and some *secondi.* The *spaghetti al rici*, spaghetti with sea urchin, looked good to me.

In came the wine.

"*Antipasti?*"

"Yes, please."

He left before I got to choose and returned with two heaping plates of richly flavored *caponata, pomodori ai anchughe* — tomatoes with anchovies, green squash marinated in tomato sauce and black olives, and a basket of flattish-looking bread sprinkled with sesame seeds that seems to be "the bread" in Sicily.

"Delisiozo," I said, giving a thumbs-up to the woman behind the counter.

She beamed me a smile. The man returned.

"Spaghetti ai rici?" I asked.

"No, no spaghetti ai rici. Pesce a la barbecue?"

Barbecued fish? I don't think so.

"How about some pasta?"

He went back to confer with the woman. Their hands went crazy since they had lots to talk about. He came back with more wine.

"Spaghetti ai vongole?" he said, opening and closing his hands to demonstrate clams.

"OK."

As I watched the woman cook them, the gentlemen at the other table finished their wine and started singing. They took our picture, then came to take selfies with us. By the time we got to exchanging emails, the pasta was ready.

Our new friends gave in to the calls from home and left.

"I'm on my way, *Cara*. The traffic's horrible. What? No, I didn't stop for a drink with the boys. What's that noise? Just people in the street."

We cleaned up our plates, finished the wine, and, sated and happy, stood up to leave.

The woman came to show me her phone.

"Come back at 9?" Google Translate suggested.

A date? I didn't think so since we were both married. More likely, the time they opened for dinner. But with the day we'd had, that was too late for us, even for Thanksgiving.

"Tomorrow," I said.

That was Thanksgiving in Palermo.

22

PALERMO'S MARKETS

Our nine days in Palermo flew like the wind. If our tiny apartment was hard to find, it was even harder to leave.

We were already used to living without a dishwasher. In Palermo, we got used to living without a microwave, a coffee maker, and a washing machine. We even got used to living without TV.

But without heat?

No.

Two days into our nine, after wearing everything we owned and trying to heat the space by running hot showers and keeping on the electric oven, I broke down. Against Steve's advice (it won't work, and it will trip the breakers, he said), I bought a space heater from the electronics store around the corner. The thing is plastic, purple, and smaller than a football. It has oversized buttons that make it look like a children's toy and cost 22 euros. But it works.

Thanks to it, our life got better, and we got less grouchy. Despite the rain, I even managed to drag Steve out of the house a few times. It rains a lot in Sicily, and it's not kidding. Every time it starts, it rains like it's never going to stop. And it's nothing like that nasty, sharp November rain we get in the North Country. This rain is gloriously unchained, with thunder and lightning, flying umbrellas, and flooded streets. It's not warm, but hey — you can't have it all.

Our Palermo home sits right in the heart of the historical Capo market, one of the oldest in Palermo. It's a maze of narrow cobbled streets clogged with stalls crumbling under the weight of ruby-red *pomodori* (tomatoes); plump pepperoncini; piles of shiny black, green, and brown olives; purple *melanzane* (eggplant); and thin green squashes looking like oversized praying mantises on the prowl. And that's just the beginning.

There's the fruit: thick-skinned rough lemons; sliced pomegranates looking like royal jewels; tiny strawberries no bigger than peppercorns, each one a flavor bomb; apples in every color known to man; bumpy *melocotone* (quinces), their flesh hard as rocks; translucent amber grapes; scaly pineapples; and more styles of oranges and clementines than I can count.

Tons of fish nestle in mountains of white snow. Silver fish, red fish, white fish, dark fish, spotted fish, all artfully curved like they're about to jump back into the sea. Fat slices of shiny pink salmon sit next to translucent filets of white fish. Solid blocks of swordfish guard the severed head with its two-foot upturned nose tied to the stand. That's how the merchant proves its authenticity so he can charge 20 euros per kilo for the white flesh, so clean it's flavorless. There's salty *baccala*, dried salted cod that needs desalting and rehydrating before it can turn into a dish that only a mother could love. There are tiny dark *cozze* (mussels)*,* gray *vongole* (clams)*,* slippery squids, and floppy octopi hiding their heads under their many arms. There are little pink *gamberi* (shrimps), clawed *langoustine* (prawn), small crabs, and so much more I can't remember.

Then the meats. Plump white chickens, cut in thirds in

width instead of length, so you get two legs, the whole breast, or two wings and a back. Massive chunks of veal, so pink it looks fake. *Suino* (pork) disassembled into boneless cutlets, slippery sausages, and rolls of marbled belly wrapped around flavorful vegetables. Oily anchovies, split into ribbons and rolled around a stuffing of oregano and lemon-peel-flavored breadcrumbs soaked in lemon. Tiny *polpette* (meatballs) drenched in thick tomato sauce that Steve covets, thinking they're meat, but they insist on being fish. Thin skewers of seasoned meats and vegetables built into fragile towers sit next to the cheese-covered slices of fried *melanzane* (eggplant). And so on.

And let me be clear: I'm not talking about the *macellarias*, the butcher's shops, of which we have four within a five-minute walk that offer every cut of meat known to man, from the raw to the very seasoned and exquisitely prepared. These are just the humble market stalls you pass on your way to church.

The *pasticerias*, the pastry stores, entice you with every possible pastry you can dream of. They have golden crusty breads as big as a truck tire that they cut and sell by weight. Long, pale, sesame-sprinkled loaves and small hand rolls just right for a "*pane ca meusa*," a spleen sandwich — unless you'd rather have *trippa* (tripe). Delicate butterfly-shaped pastries loaded with *albicocca* (apricot jam); chocolate sprinkled cookies; balls of dough filled with creamy ricotta flavored with lemon zest and vanilla; twists of fluffy baked dough dripping butter, and bow-like mille-feuille powdered with sugar.

They're handy any time of the day. You down a couple with your breakfast cappuccino, a few more with the espresso that helps you beat the mid-morning slump, or grab one for dessert. Whenever you happen to feel peckish.

There are convenience stores that sell everything from wine to toilet paper. A church or two, just in case you need to get yourself right with God before lunch. Countless coffee shops and bars, handy for a quick *aperitivo* or aromatic espresso, come with exciting conversation and broad hand gestures so the third-floor deaf neighbor can participate.

Frail old ladies with red hair and white roots shuffle along, leaning on their shopping carts and checking every stall. They listen to the vendors sing praise for their goods, steal a taste, and move on like the shrewd nannas they are. Zippy scooters zoom from stall to stall, slipping on the wet cobbles, the space under the feet piled high with bags.

Plump cats who bristle when touched investigate the fish. Dogs roam the streets, from fashionable springers sporting hooded red Christmas coats and boots to nondescript strays. But if you think street dogs are a scourge, you're wrong. Here, every dog has his place. They belong to the community.

We were having lunch at a market restaurant watching Dada, the shaggy orange resident dog, guarding the *macellaria*.

A large black dog stopped by Dada and politely offered his butt for sniffing. Dada wagged her tail and let him in. Minutes later, he came out with his tail held high, carrying a massive cow femur.

The skinny dog that came next had a soft, hanging belly. She'd left her puppies at home to do her shopping. Dada allowed her in, and Skinny returned with the butcher, who gave her a bag of leftovers and watched her eat.

After a while, Dada got antsy and bullied her way to the bag. The butcher pushed her aside to let the mom eat.

Palermo's markets are the beating heart of the city. They're the place to be social; catch up with the gossip; have a snack, a coffee, or a drink; go to church; show off your new hairdo; or try out your new scooter. And if all else fails, you can even buy stuff.

23

LEAVING PALERMO

LEAVING PALERMO WAS BITTERSWEET. We'd spent nine days cooped-up in a minuscule apartment, listening to the rain and working on the last touches for my book *K-9 Lovely*. At times it felt like a lot. But when the rain stopped and we went outside, we had a blast! I loved the chaos of the markets, the people speaking with their hands, the cars so banged up they were narrower than they had started. I loved living in the very heart of the city, so I could come and go as I pleased a dozen times a day. And boy, was it fun to ditch the car for a week!

Besides editing, formatting, and fussing with manuscripts, we did some touristy things. I visited the former royal palace, now the site of the Sicilian Parliament. Don't bother. It's a rip-off. Thirteen euros bought me access to Purification, a modern art exhibition featuring mostly people hanging by their wrists or drowning under waterfalls to cleanse themselves. They should have tried a colonic. And the incessant noise of running water got me desperate for a toilet.

The royal apartments were closed, so I only saw the Royal Chapel, a gilded prayer den the size of a large elevator chock full of Byzantine mosaics. And I didn't even have Steve with me to complain to. He'd brought along his Swiss Army knife with a dull blade shorter than my pinkie, a nail file, and a tweezer, so he was deemed dangerous and denied entry.

I can't but agree. He's known to be sneaky. Who knows whose nails he'd manage to file and impede the workings of the Sicilian democracy? Happy to be off the hook, he chilled under the palm trees while I delighted in the exhibits. Lucky him!

We left the palace to see the city. We walked into some free churches and around some paying ones, wondering how many people broke their backs to build them a thousand years ago. We toured *Teatro Maximo*, the second largest theatre in the world, listened to the orchestra practicing *La Boheme*, and talked to ourselves to check out the acoustics. Even better, we got to sit in the red velvet royal balcony, where they filmed the end of *Godfather 3*.

We twisted our ankles over cobblestones, admired the daring graffiti, and tried the grappa. That's THE Italian spirit made from grape skins that can give *pálinka*, the Transylvanian double-distilled plum brandy, a run for its money. We counted the missing body parts at the Fountain of Shame in Piazza Pretoria, a spectacular marble fountain whose naked statues scandalized the nuns at the nearby monastery.

To cover the shameful nakedness, the nuns dressed them in clothes. The locals stole the clothes. When all else failed, a bunch of stealthy nuns came out at night armed with hammers and chisels and amputated the offensive body parts. The authorities built a fence around the fountain to protect what was left. It's still there today.

Hand in hand, we joined hundreds of other couples in the *passegiatta*, the ritual evening walk when everyone ambles around to see and be seen, crowding the streets before dinner. We window-shopped for Sicilian dog fashions, so I can tell you that hoodies are hot. So are pockets and three-quarter sleeves on all four legs.

We admired the well-dressed locals sipping hot chocolate in the freezing wind-swept piazzas.

We did it all, but the last day finally came. Time to go.

We started by dropping the garbage off with the neighbors.

I may have forgotten to mention, but Palermo's garbage management takes some getting used to, especially after Sardinia, where recycling is a religion.

Palermo doesn't recycle. In fact, after two weeks in Palermo, I can state with complete confidence that the only way to get rid of the trash is to tie it in a plastic bag and drop it in the street.

It took me a while to wrap my head around that, but it's true. It's embarrassing and not pretty, but it somehow works. The garbage fairy comes at night to clean the garbage piles so people can rebuild them in the morning.

Sadly, thanks to pigeons, cats, and other creatures I shall not name, the bags get broken into and gutted, and the contents get scattered around the neighborhood. Not pretty. But, surprisingly, it doesn't smell. Nor does the market, despite the garbage, the fish, and everything else. Maybe because of December's chill and endless rain?

I wish I could say the same about the back streets. Here in Sicily, public toilets are rare, so dark alleys smell like human debris. But otherwise, the air is clean, the sky is blue, and life is fantastic. But I digress.

We dropped the garbage with the neighbors, then packed everything we owned, from the extra rolls of toilet paper to the purple space heater. We dragged ourselves to the car that Steve had gladly abandoned in an underground parking lot nine days before. Thankfully, we found it. We loaded our stuff and got ready to go.

That's when Steve discovered he'd thrown the parking ticket in the garbage, so we couldn't get out. We had to get it back.

We went to recover the garbage, but the pile had grown.

Steve shooed away a few indignant cats looking for free-bies. They hissed but backed off. They could see the man was on a mission. He started rummaging bare-handed amongst Pepsi bottles, yogurt containers, vegetable leftovers, and other things best left unnamed.

"Is this ours?" he asked, grabbing a bag full of wine bottles.

"Not this one. The blue one."

We took it home under the keen eyes of a third-floor elderly lady who must have had her eye on it. We rummaged through it until we found the parking ticket. Steve wiped it with toilet paper and slipped it in his pocket, then we dropped back the garbage and headed to the car.

On the way out, I stopped by the next-door *enoteca* to buy two bottles of wine. The way we'd started, we'd need them soon. The pleasant young lady asked me if I wanted to consume them on the spot — it was almost 10 a.m. after all — or take them away. That's how I knew that our reputation had preceded us.

"I'll take them away," I said.

She packed them and handed me the bill.

I handed her my credit card.

She frowned.

"No cash?"

"Not enough. Maybe if you give me a discount…"

She shook her head and took me down the road. Steve, seated at a table outside, watched me leave with wary eyes.

"Where are you going?"

"To pay," I said.

The restaurant down the street charged my card. I took

custody of the wine and returned to get Steve, who looked like he needed a drink.

On the way to the car, we passed by the sandwich cart, and I invested three euros in a hot tripe sandwich sprinkled with oregano and a squeeze of lemon juice. I'd barely taken two bites when the used bookstore's resident dog ambushed me. I'm fond of bookish dogs, so I gave him the rest of my sandwich. He grabbed it and ran inside. The bookseller shot me an ugly glare. I guess he wanted some too.

Back to the garage, Steve went to get the car, and I went to pay. But the machine didn't like any of my credit cards. Bummer.

It was Sunday morning, with no attendant in sight. I sighed, cursed in a heartfelt Romanian, and paid 90 euros in cash. That was almost all I had, but it was better than getting stuck in the parking lot until Monday.

We squeezed out of Palermo through the narrow streets choked with double-parked cars flashing their lights as usual. I fleetingly wondered if they had extra batteries to keep them going until they finished their business. We ended our Palermo visit just like we started, in utter chaos.

But what fun!

24

TRAVELING

Traveling opens your mind. There's magic in taking the road less traveled, even if others have traveled it a thousand times. To you, it's new. So's everything you see and learn.

But the magic of travel goes beyond seeing new places, people, and things. Traveling forces you to question your assumptions and opens your mind. You don't think so? I'll show you. Let's start with food.

Rich or poor, Republican or Democrat, intelligent or dull, we all eat, no matter our color, age, religion, or sexual orientation. Food is the fuel that keeps us going, a sensual pleasure, a social activity, a shared cultural experience, an adventure, and sometimes a curse — just think about Thanksgiving with the in-laws. From humans to caterpillars, food is something we can all relate to. We all have beliefs about food — starting with what IS food and what is not. Locusts, crickets, and scorpions may be food to some, but not to you. On the other hand, things you think of as food — like a juicy steak, fried bacon, rice crackers, and root beer — may be as repugnant to others as fried bamboo worms are to you.

But let's leave aside the extremes and talk about the basics.

Let's take pizza. It's about as basic and familiar as it gets, isn't it? It's a disk of baked dough sprinkled with all sorts of stuff, including cheese, that gets cut into triangular slices and eaten hot. It makes a good lunch, an excellent snack, and sometimes even dinner.

But is it?

Now that we're in Italy, the cradle of pizza, we've discovered that much of what we thought we knew about pizza was wrong. Here it goes:

1. Pizza is not lunch food. Pizza is dinner. So much so that in Italy, most pizzerias don't even open for lunch. They'll light the woodfire by six; if you're lucky, you may get to eat by seven. Not before. That's why whenever someplace offers pizza for lunch — for foreigners, of course — they make a big stink about it. "Here we have pizza, even for lunch," they'll spell in giant letters like it's a big deal. Because it is. Italian lunch is a complicated affair that takes hours and includes *antipasti*, *primi*, *secondi*, and *dolci*. And stimulating conversation and vino, of course. Pizza? That's just dinner.

2. Pizza does not get cut into triangular slices. Sometimes it's squares, sometimes rhomboids, sometimes it comes in sheets, and more often than not, it doesn't get cut at all. You get a big pizza pie, a knife, and a fork, and there you go. Eat. You're a big boy. Or girl. You should be able to cut your food.

3. Pizza can have whatever toppings it wants, from the usual to the unusual. It can have clams, mussels, Gorgonzola cheese, or fries. Hotdogs, anyone? Shrimp? Cabbage? Pizza is an art form, and the sky's the limit.

4. Unlike many other relationships, pizza does not get shared. Italian pizzas are monogamous.

5. Pizza is not hand food. It requires a fork and a knife.

And the list goes on. There's no end to the assumptions that can get you in trouble.

Let's speak about *secondi* — that's the main dish in Italy, and it's called *secondo* because it comes after the *primo*, which is pasta more often than not, and after the *antipasto*, which comes — you guessed it — before the pasta.

In America, the main dish always comes with at least one side dish, sometimes two or three, and often with a salad you didn't even think to order. Here, in Sicily, if you order a beef steak, you get just that. A beef steak, sitting lonely and forlorn on her plate, feeling sorry for herself. There are no fries, baked potatoes, mac and cheese, pickles, onion rings, or anything. Salad? Are you kidding? If you want it, you'd better order it. And pay for it, of course.

If you want ice in your Coke, ask for it. If you want butter with your toast, order it. If you like cheese in your omelet — or in anything else, for that matter — you'd better ask for it, or you'll just get the dizzy eggs.

25

A BAD DAY IN TRAPANI

TODAY WENT BAD. But let me start from the beginning.

We couldn't believe the notices stuck up and down the street telling us the electricity would be off from 8:45 to 4:30. Are you kidding me? With no electricity, there'll be no internet, no light, no fridge, no heat, no nothing. That can't be real!

But it was.

What do we do?

We could go out in the rain — it's been raining for two days in Trapani, and today looks no different.

We could stay in and spend the day in the dark since our ground-floor flat has tiny windows that let in less light than you'd get in a doghouse.

We ended up driving up the mountain overlooking the port of Trapani to visit Erice, Trapani's twin medieval village. That turned out to be a charming place with too many churches and too few toilets.

Centuries ago, Trapani used to be just Erice's tiny port. But history had its say. These days, Trapani is a bustling port with a population of seventy thousand that ditched its tuna fishing and coral work for tourism, while Erice stood frozen in time on top of its mountain, holding on to its history, cobblestones, and churches.

The ride up the mountain was exhilarating. Hairpin after hairpin of narrow roads leaning over the cliff reminded us of the never-ending excitement of Corsica. Add to that the sun switching to rain and back every five minutes, the sheep grazing on the green slopes, and the endless allure of the fixer-uppers with fantastic views calling on you to give them a new life.

We stopped for a lovely long walk on a rocky mule path that hugged the mountain. We gazed at the blinking sea down below and wondered about the blackened trees and bushes that had survived a recent fire. We struggled to take selfies in the gusts of wind, admired the fluttery purple irises, and watched the fleshy carnivorous plants enticing their dinner. Then the rain came out of the blue, and we rushed back to the car.

We made it to the top. We took in the troubled sea; the profusion of cats cursing at each other; the moody old towers; and the steep, narrow cobblestoned streets. It was glorious.

We climbed up the old tower's worn steps to count its six bells, bending over to avoid the low ceilings. We went from church to church, taking in the harrowing paintings of tortured martyrs and the lifelike painted statues. We squinted to read the old tombstones worn by thousands of steps and soaked up the sun on the crenelated walls.

All in all, we had a splendid time while being true to ourselves. Steve figured out the construction details, checked the electric panels, and evaluated the fuses in every church we entered. I pondered the medical management of the martyrs' injuries and figured out the medieval prostheses and mobility aids. Awesome fun!

Feeling good about our day, we drove down the same heart-stopping hairpins and stopped to see the lovely sailboat Steve coveted. Then we tried our luck for a table at a nearby, highly recommended restaurant.

We were in luck.

We ordered the local wine and the famous local dish — fish *brodo*, which happens to be plain couscous smelling like fish.The wine was lovely, but my *brodo* was not. I eyed Steve's fries and his seafood, wondering how to con him into a switch.

Then Steve faded.

I could see he wasn't well, even though he said nothing — he seldom does. He pushed his plate aside, then lowered his head on the table.

"Are you OK?" I asked.

He shook his head.

"Does anything hurt?"

"I don't feel good," he said.

He closed his eyes and shivered. He shook all over, then slid off his chair.

I jumped and caught him before he fell on the floor, just as the waiter brought my *secondo*. He saw us on the floor and paled.

I checked Steve's pulse. It was good. He was breathing.

He was pale and clammy but alive.

More waiters arrived.

"Should we call an ambulance?"

"No, thanks. We'll be alright."

Steve opened his eyes.

I searched his pockets for the keys to our apartment, which was only two minutes away. I couldn't find them.

Steve slumped back.

I rummaged through his pants and found the keys.

"We can call you an ambulance in a moment," the waiter said.

"No, thanks. Can I pay, please? We need to go."

I dropped the money on the table, helped a dazed Steve into his coat, and supported him out under the waiters' worried gaze.

"Your food?"

"I'll be back."

We shuffled to the flat. I laid Steve down, examined him, and put him to bed.

He walks and speaks alright. He has no deficits in his hands or legs to make me worry about a stroke. He has no headache to make me suspect a bleed. He has no recent trauma, drug use, or withdrawal, and he had a glass and a half of wine, which is no problem for him. He hasn't been sick, and he took his medications. And he has no history of seizures, but I know without a shadow of a doubt that that's precisely what he had.

If we were home, and he was my patient, I'd get him a CT scan, a slew of blood tests, an MRI, an EEG, and a neurology consult. After all that, we'd have a fifty-fifty chance of having a diagnosis. High on the list are a tumor, a stroke, and an electrolyte abnormality.

And there's a fifty-fifty chance we wouldn't.

Either way, he'd have to start taking medications, stop driving, and forget about doing risky things. The things that are his life.

That might help. Or not.

But we're not home.

We're thousands of miles away from home in Trapani, Sicily. We have one more night in this rented apartment we vacate tomorrow to drive someplace we don't know that's hundreds of miles away.

My beloved husband, the strongest man I know, lies beside me, and he doesn't even remember what happened.

What do I do?
I don't know.
We'll have to talk.
But for now, he wants ice cream.
I'll go get him some.

26

THE TRIP TO AGRIGENTO

WE TALKED. Steve wanted no check-up, no hospital, and no going home. He understood the risks but wanted to go on. So that's what we did.

Like every other day in Sicily, it rained when we left Trapani. We gathered our stuff, starting with the grappa and our space heater, which had gone to the top of the list of things we can't do without — ahead of toilet paper, shampoo, and even coffee. We packed everything in our car that no longer looked new after two months of incessant travels through weird places and headed south to Agrigento's Valley of the Temples.

We stopped at Segesta, an old elysian ruin gracing a glorious hillside setting. Twenty-five hundred years later, the Greek temple in the valley is still unfinished. Talk about slow contractors!

The rough, thick columns are made of massive stone disks stacked on top of each other like ultra-thick pancakes. They're sturdy and built to last, but they lack the elaborate capitals and the uplifting grace of the Acropolis. The Elysians, an ancient people nobody knows much about since Google translate hasn't yet gotten to their language, built it as a PR stunt to enlist the Athenians' help against the Carthaginian threat.

"We are your people. We're just like you. Come defend us," the temple was meant to say.

But the Athenians were busy getting their asses kicked by the Spartans, so the Carthaginians wiped out the Elysians, leaving behind nothing but the unfinished temple and an amphitheater up the hill. That two-thousand-year-old amphitheater is so well designed that its excellent acoustics allowed me to blast "*Sono Italiano*," "I'm Italian," to the two thousand empty stone seats. They loved it.

Steve didn't. That's why all the pictures he took of my concert went blurry.

We got rained on three times on our hike up the hill. Fortunately, Steve had his raincoat for once — I practically sleep in mine — and it was worth it. We even got a rainbow!

We returned to the car to find a brochure advertising lunch at a nearby *agriturismo* — one of the many Italian farms that supplement their income by offering food and beds to the tourists. And, since we're always ready for adventure, we decided to try it.

We started doubting our wisdom when we left the main road for a washed-out dirt road. Did I mention that it rains in Sicily? We crawled under a graffiti-covered bridge, then up a slippery, muddy hill between vines and cacti, and started getting weary. Were we being set up to get robbed? Would it be wiser to stick to the cookies and tea, which were all we had left?

But wisdom is seldom on our menu, so we went on. We drove for miles, dropping from pothole to pothole until we found the place. And what a place that was!

A handsome stone building looking over vines, with landscaped gardens and a fountain sussuring on the porch. The restaurant was rustic and lovely, with a dozen white-cloth tables, half of them taken by impatient customers harassing the haggard-looking staff.

Like everywhere else in Sicily, there was no menu; there was just a QR code on the table. Because of Covid or love of progress, paper menus in Italy went the way of dinosaurs.

No matter how hard we tried, we couldn't get the Wi-Fi password to work to scan the QR code, so the waiter brought us a paper English menu. House wine, 6 euros/liter. Quail, 4 euros each. Pizzas, 4 to 8 euros each. All looking great.

We sipped on the decent house red and watched the waiters bring steamy plates to other tables. Our food came, and it was delicious. Steve had a *quattro gusto pizza*, which was not a *quattro stagioni,* and went a bit heavy on the hot dogs. I had the mouth-watering *pappardelle ala cinghiale,* wide pasta with wild boar ragu. We shared a juicy roasted quail and a skewered *stigghiolla* I'd ordered just for the mouthwatering name. It turned out to be lamb intestines rolled around a leek and grilled into golden deliciousness. We finished with a freshly filled *cannolo* — they get soggy if they wait — rolled in nuts, and coffee. Espresso, of course — that's what you get here when you order coffee. We each got a full teaspoon of it, strong enough to make our teeth clatter.

Thus sated, we asked for the bill. I'd calculated it ahead of time, like I always do, at under 39 euros.

Surprise, surprise — it was 47. Each item was charged 1–2 euros more than on the menu. The 6-euro liter of house wine turned out to be 8 euros for 750 milliliters.

That bill didn't taste good.

It wasn't expensive — the food was delicious and worth it. We'd have gladly paid that for it, but we felt taken. So did the woman at the following table, who was charged for two glasses of wine when she only had one.

So we did get robbed — just not at gunpoint.

That made us sad.

Then Steve had an idea.

"What if the English menus they gave us had the old prices? What if those were the actual prices on the QR codes?"

I hoped he was right. We still didn't get what we ordered, but I'd love it to be a mistake rather than cheating.

I couldn't wait to get online and check.

They had a great website. Lots of pictures of the place, the rooms, the food. But they wisely left out the prices.

Multiple TripAdvisor reviews mention getting overcharged. What a pity!

On our way to Agrigento, we stopped for gas, which is always a hassle. We only manage to get gas every third try since the pumps don't like our credit cards, despite their bells and whistles and chips and pins.

It was dark by the time we got to Agrigento. As usual, our place was in the old downtown, so we got lost on the cobbled streets looking for it. Thanks to good old Gwendolyn, we got into a lane so narrow that Steve had to fold the mirrors. He was still pushing through with an inch on each side between the car and the stone buildings when the locals stopped us.

"The street gets too narrow. Back up."

We didn't believe the first man, nor the second, but when the fourth person said the same, we decided we'd better.

But how? How do you back up without mirrors between rough stone buildings with an inch on each side?

"Try the backup camera," a man said. Men! They always know.

Steve disagreed.

"The backup camera is fixed in the car's center and doesn't see its corners."

The locals stared as I did my best to guide him out. They called their neighbors. Some went late to their dates to watch us. A young family had their dinner get cold. Someone said a bride missed her wedding, but I think they exaggerated. It must have been just the engagement since I saw no white brides. And who on earth gets married at six in the evening?

Either way, we had an audience any stand-up comedian would cherish. Then a cat chose that precise moment to get under the car and cause further trouble like cats always do.

The tension was thick, the stakes high. I'll never forget the stone walls, the darkness, the onlookers, and the bleeping sensors at all four corners of the car blaring like crazy. And the cat.

But Steve got us out without a scratch. There was widespread cheering and clapping, though the cat looked pissed. What a hero!

We eventually made it to our new home by the cathedral, even though it had no number, sign, or any other distinguishing feature than a "*Vendesi,*" "For sale," sign above the gate.

We carried our stuff up four floors of marble steps to our new digs that featured a bed, a table, and a sofa but no windows. And no heat.

Boy, did that grappa taste good!

27

AGRIGENTO

REACHING AGRIGENTO, the Greekest of Sicilian cities, wasn't easy, but it was worth it.

Our first day in Agrigento consisted of a 15-kilometer walk. We journeyed to — and shuffled back from — the famous Valley of Temples. That's pretty much the only, albeit glorious, remnant of a flourishing Greek city that rivaled Athens in 500 BC.

The old town of Akragas had at least eight temples dedicated to various gods to suit every need, taste, or situation. Unlike today's monotheist religions, where the one and only God has to address every aspect of human life, Greeks had specialized gods to deal with every situation. Do you need luck with hunting? Sacrifice to Artemis, the hunt goddess. You're hurting in love? Check with Aphrodite. Do you need to win a war? Call on Ares, the Greek god of war. You're lacking in wisdom? First, you're probably doing fine since only wise people know their limitations. Have you heard about the Dunning-Kruger effect? If not, this is what *Britannica* has to say about it:

"Dunning-Kruger effect, in psychology, is a cognitive bias

whereby people with limited knowledge greatly overestimate their competence in that domain relative to objective criteria or to the performance of their peers." As in, they're too stupid to know it.

But I digress again. If you need wisdom, Athena, the goddess of wisdom, crafts, and skilled peacetime pursuits, is your go-to.

The Valley of Temples is a 1,300-hectare archeological park featuring a plethora of ancient ruins. It's the remnant of a Greek city complete with homes, markets, roads, aqueducts, and gardens that got wiped out by the Carthaginians in 406 BCE. What pests, those Carthaginians!

Later cultures, from the Romans to the Christians, scavenged the remnants and used the stone to build their own cities. But there's still enough left to move your soul and fill your mind with wonder. How could a bunch of people who've been dead for almost three thousand years build something like this when we, in the computer era, can't even fix the potholes in our roads?

We wandered between the sunbaked golden sandstone columns, whose painted plaster got stripped by Sicily's wind and rains long ago. We wondered at the 18-foot-tall atlases called telamons, who used to support the massive temple of Zeus on their heads. The broken columns, thick enough to hide a grown man, are now just a pile of rocks. We feasted our hungry eyes on the hundred-year-old olive trees. We gawked at the fragrant oranges bending the branches in the shady gardens of Kolymbethra. Then we headed home, looking for a lunch place.

But we were late.

In Sicily, all self-respecting restaurants, and most of the others, close between 2:30 and 7 p.m. But of course! Who'd ever think to eat before seven?

So we climbed mile after mile toward our place up the hill, keeping our eyes peeled for anything looking like food. But it happened to be the day the Sicilians celebrate the Immaculate Conception, so everything was closed — shops, supermarkets, banks, pharmacies.

To take my mind off my hunger, I started calculating how the Immaculate Conception occurring on December 8 could possibly result in the divine birth on December 25, but I didn't get far. Maybe because I didn't have a pregnancy wheel.

By the time we got home, I had lost any hope of finding food. But, much to my delight, I discovered that the next-door *pasticeria* was open. I walked in just as the owner brought an oblong pizza the size of a SMART car out of the oven.

"I'll have some," I said.

He grabbed a pair of shears. I stepped back.

"*Tanto?*" This much? he asked, indicating about a square foot.

"*Si. Due,*" Yes. Two of them.

He cut the pizza with the scissors, weighed it, wrapped it, and handed it to me in exchange for nine euros. That was some of the best money I ever spent to save my sanity and our marriage.

We climbed the four floors to our place, grabbed a bottle of wine, then sat on the terrace, watching the sunset over Port Empedocle and dreaming about settling in Agrigento. We could live on cheap pizza and sepia-black *Nero di Avola* in a condo overlooking the Mediterranean. We'd walk up and down those hills until our legs shortened, then we'd hem our pants.

Then we remembered that we weren't there to settle; we were there to explore. Our home was the journey. So we moved on.

The next day we took an easy ride to the magnificent *Villa Romana Dei Casale*, the luxurious two-thousand-year-old home of a wealthy Roman merchant. Thanks to a massive landslide 600 years ago, its marvelous mosaics were preserved from destruction and looting until their recent discovery a few decades ago.

The owner is believed to have been a wild animal trader. What sort of business is that, you ask? A very lucrative one, in fact. Poor Romans, they didn't have Facebook or TikTok. Not even cell phones or cable. So, to keep themselves entertained, they watched fights — the wilder, the better. Lions, tigers, bears, and gladiators were granted the privilege of spilling each other's blood to entertain the masses. But they didn't last long. So, in comes our friend, the animal trader, to supply more, satisfy the market, and get rich.

We took pictures of the splendid two-thousand-year-old mosaics of tigers, bears, dolphins, and dancers, looking like they were made yesterday thought to be used as catalogs for buyers.

We marveled at the bikini ladies playing the first beach volleyball tournament. We stared at the lady in the golden peplum whose wardrobe malfunction got recorded for eternity. We wondered at the kids racing bird-pulled chariots. Would you have your toddler driving a goose-powered cart? Only if he made you really, really mad. I lusted over the thermae, wishing I could have a nice hot soak. Oh, how I miss home! But I digress again.

On the way home, we stopped for lunch at a well-recommended restaurant.

It didn't look like much. A tiny house under a highway bridge surrounded by a chicken wire fence, minus the chickens.

Rain fell over us in sheets as we circled the building looking for a way in. The first door lacked a handle. The one by the entrance sign was locked, despite the half dozen cars parked nearby.

We were ready to leave when a harried man carrying a plastic bag headed to the rear of the house and opened a humble back door. Funny way to get into an expensive restaurant, I thought, but I was too hungry to care. I tried to follow him, but he stopped me.

"Not for you. You there."

He pointed to the locked door.

I went back. Steve shrugged and headed to the car.

I shook the door. I knocked. I was considering breaking it down when I noticed the doorbell.

I rang, even though I'd never eaten in a locked restaurant. But for that one time in Portugal…

A young man in a long white apron, looking like an over-sized cricket, opened the door.

"Food?" I said.

He called me in.

"Just a second."

I stuck my head out but kept my foot in so he couldn't close the door and called Steve.

He ambled in more calmly than I cared for.

"You have reservations?" the cricket asked.

"No."

I thought he'd throw us out, but he got a ledger instead.

"Your name?"

"Jones."

"Your phone number?"

My phone number? But I'm right here!

But I was hungry. So I had Steve look for the phone number of our French phone. It's my old broken phone Steve fixed with duct tape. We've been using it for months but still can't remember the number.

"Wait."

He left and returned with an imposing woman who checked

our health passes — like they do at every restaurant — and led us to a table by the wood-burning fireplace. The room was comfortable, elegant, and understated, just fit for a Michelin-starred restaurant.

We chose the lunch special and the house wine. They were good, especially the wine. We waited for our food, watching the chef, a rotund man like Jacques Pepin, court this *bon vivant* that looked like Pavarotti who tried dish after dish.

They discussed the ingredients' delicacy and the preparation's intricacy as we ate our way through the *amuse-bouche* featuring kale, grilled *melanzana al mellograno* (eggplant with pomegranate,) pasta, and dessert, while everyone ignored us.

Steve and I made bets. Is he a food critic? They're too familiar. An old friend? Not familiar enough. A potential investor? More likely, since Covid put a damper on tourism all over Italy. The chef poured himself a glass of wine and took a seat. They were still talking as we left, and I wished my Italian was good enough to eavesdrop. But I consoled myself that they talked about food. That's what everyone talks about in Sicily, even us.

The sun was setting as we headed home. We took a dirt road to avoid a road closure, but the torrential rains had done a job on the road. The mud got deeper and deeper, and the cars vanished. All but one that looked stuck in the mud a hundred feet ahead.

We stopped, and I got out to see if they needed help. My sneakers got heavier with mud with every step.

Americans, of course. The road had gotten so bad they wanted to turn around, but they feared getting stuck. Could we wait to see them out?

Of course.

I clomped to our car and tried to shake the mud off my feet, but it resisted.

Oh well. I scraped some of it with a stick and took the rest in.

We waited for them to leave, then turned around and headed home. The trip was long and slow, but we made it. We even found a place to park — thanks, Athena, goddess of skillful peaceful pursuits.

We were too pooped for anything else but a shower, yesterday's pizza leftovers, and sleep.

But we'd made it through another day.

28

DRIVERS AND DRIVING

SICILIANS ARE LOVELY PEOPLE. Friendly, caring, smiling, and always ready to help. Until they get behind the wheel.

Then, they turn into maniacal demons and stop making sense.

We got stuck behind a long row of cars at an exit. It took forever to get out and see the reason: two cars that wouldn't give way. Trouble, I thought, expecting the two drivers who had caused the blockage to fight when they got out of their cars. But, instead of shooting each other, they embraced and kissed.

Steve and I stared at them, then at each other. Were they making up after an accident? Were they long-lost friends finally getting together? Were they attending the same funeral, expressing condolences? We didn't know. What we did know, though, is that no one blew their horn. No one. And here, they blow their horn for everything, from someone blowing a stop sign to someone taking too long to take off after a red light. I bet wearing the wrong shade of lipstick is a blowable offense in Sicily — but not blocking traffic to hug. So there.

Steve was miffed.

"What the heck? They're always blowing their horn at us, and half of the time, I don't even know why," he said.

I tried to be encouraging.

"Maybe it's not for us?"

Steve shrugged. Who knows? But as we approach the mainland, the horn blows become even more frequent. The drivers can't help but congratulate each other for their excellent driving with suggestive hand gestures and vigorous horn blows. Maybe because here street signs are merely suggestions, STOP signs are optional, and the lines... What lines?

"What's the difference between a single uninterrupted line and a double uninterrupted line?" I asked.

"You can't pass," Steve said.

"Yes, but what's the difference?"

Steve shrugged.

"The single uninterrupted line you can pass if you're Italian. It carries the exact same weight as a STOP sign."

I think he made that up. But I'm not sure.

"How about using the turn signal?" I asked, watching a car hook a stealthy left.

Steve shrugged.

"You don't want to use the turn signal. The other drivers will know where you're going and get an unfair advantage. Plus, the Maseratis have different road rights. No other car can ignore the road signs the same way."

I thought he was kidding.

"How about the vegetable-loaded Tuk-Tuk we almost hit this morning?" I asked.

"He was asserting his Maserati rights."

He shrugged. "And look at the speed limit. It's 50. I'm going 120, and I can't keep up."

The drivers aren't the only ones being rude. Some of the traffic signs would offend American drivers.

"You want my parking spot? Take my handicap too," reads the sign over a disabled parking space.

The Driver's Take:

The last few times we visited Italy, I observed the drivers and vowed to never drive here. But that vow went out the window when we leased a car for our European driving vacation.

At least we were able to ease into Italian driving. We picked up the car in Paris and drove to southern France before boarding the ferry to Corsica. France has thousands of rotary intersections (roundabouts). These can have one, two, or three concentric, counterclockwise lanes. There appears to be a definite lane usage rule that I never learned properly, so I was frequently the subject of horns blaring. It seems you should signal right and enter the outer lane ONLY if you plan to take the first exit. For any other exit, you should signal left and enter an inner parallel lane until your exit comes up. Then you signal right and move over. Unfortunately, we often got trapped on the inside, and I had to perform a few extra circuits to get out.

So I learned to stay in the outer lane, to the annoyance of French drivers who used the roundabout correctly.

After the ferry from Provence, Corsica was a good transition to Italian driving. Corsica is officially a province of France, but Corsicans are neither French nor Italian. They are somewhere in between. Corsican mountain roads are nothing but switchback turns that the locals take on two wheels. We continuously built a line of cars behind us, so we took every occasion to pull off to let them pass. They expressed their appreciation with a toot or flash of taillights. Roundabouts are fewer in Corsica, and rules are more casual.

The Italian island of Sardinia is a short ferry ride from

Corsica, but it's thoroughly Italian from a driving perspective. The Sardinian drivers don't acknowledge when you move out of their way. The side roads are usually one chariot wide, with cars parked along both sides. Cars entering the main road from a side alley usually pull way out into the travel lane to get a sight line and intimidate the passing traffic to let them in.

The ocean-going ferries are quite different from the two-way commuter ferries crossing Lake Champlain. Ocean ferries load and unload only at the bow. There may be two ramps, but they're both at the bow (or both at the stern). Operators turn vehicles around when loading, so they head in the correct direction for disembarkation. Still, sometimes they load them facing aft, then turn them individually to unload.

In Sicily, the driving gets even crazier. Stop signs are totally ignored, and roundabouts are a free-for-all. Sicily's motorways between cities introduced us to Italian highway driving. In Italy, the left lane is for overtaking only. Cars coming from behind seem to have the right-of-way when passing on the left, even if you're overtaking a slower vehicle or exceeding the speed limit. They'll roar up behind you, flashing their headlights, demanding you get the hell out of their way.

There appears to be a rigid hierarchy of brand rights-of-way. Audis take precedence over Fiats, Mercedes and BMWs take precedence over Audis, and Porsches and Maseratis trump BMWs and everything else but Ferraris or Lamborghinis.

A short ferry ride from Sicily lands you in southern Italy, where the mountains are sprinkled with hill towns that all have chariot-wide streets. We would have been better off with a smaller car so we wouldn't have to keep folding our mirrors to pass through.

The driving gets even more serious in Italy proper. The motorways have tolls, but every toll booth uses a different payment process. Some require immediate payment as you pass.

Some entail taking a ticket and paying as you exit. Others involve no payment at all but just passing through the toll both.

Gasoline is another matter. Many gas stations are unattended with automatic payment kiosks. Unfortunately, our U.S. credit cards didn't always work because of some embedded PIN discrepancy. We often had to search out the attended stations where they could use a different type of card reader. That often had us driving on fumes.

In southern and central Italy, we drove mostly on secondary roads. Driving at or slightly above the speed limit often required us to pull over to let impatient drivers pass.

Speed limits in Europe are posted as black numerals in a red circle. Our car had a forward-facing camera that recognized the posted limit and displayed it on the instrument panel. The posted limits in France make sense. In Corsica and Sardinia, the limits on the mountain switchbacks are typically higher than you can safely travel at, other than a rally car. In Sicily and Italy proper, the posted limits appear to fluctuate randomly, which totally confuses the in-car display.

Parking is a disaster throughout, but nowhere worse than in the hill towns of Italy. Our lease car is a full-size SUV — the only model they had. The locals mostly drive cars half this size, and it's not unusual for them to park diagonally in a tiny parallel space with their back end sticking into the road.

Driving in Italy is the worst. Local drivers enter the main roads, at speed, from parking lots and side streets, seemingly daring you to hit them. If eye contact convinces them that you won't back down, they'll panic and brake partway across the intersection. You need to bob and weave into oncoming traffic to avoid them.

29

RAGUSA

RAGUSA IS nothing like Sicily's other cities. First, it's a twin, so there are two Ragusas.

Ragusa *Ibla*, the old city, was built on the side of a mountain. Its narrow, crooked lanes wrap around each other like vines, crippling the high-heeled fashionistas. The whole *Ibla* squeezes between its thick stone walls, all that's left from the cataclysmic 1693 earthquake that razed the city. Today's *Ibla* is barely 300 years old, rebuilt by those who couldn't afford to start over elsewhere. Its tiny, thick-walled homes speak of history and tradition.

Ragusa *Superiore*, the new town, was built on the nearby slope of a higher hill. It looks down upon its older twin like a successful younger brother looking at its less fortunate sibling with both superiority and love.

Ragusa *Superiore's* narrow lanes are a tad straighter, her buildings a bit newer, and its car access just this side of terrible. *Ibla's* lanes are fewer and more crooked, its parking lots nonexistent, and its shops — what shops?

But when all is said and done, the two are peas from the same pod. The streets are too narrow for two cars, the parking is pathetic, and the uneven cobblestones force you to watch your feet. Oodles of well-fed, haughty free cats roam the walls, looking at you down their noses. As for the paths that the Ragusans call streets, no one in their right mind would call them so. They're nothing but long strings of stone steps alternating with pedestrian-only lanes, too steep and too narrow for cars.

Once in a while, you'll find yourself in a tunnel ducking under a drivable street or stuck between two buildings leaning toward each other. But for the most part, the whole of Ragusa is nothing but a maze of narrow, steep steps, making me wish I'd called my outdoor walk a stair stepper workout.

On Google, walking from one Ragusa to the other is a piece of cake. That's because maps don't do 3D. I'd be fine walking on that map, cobblestones and all, if it weren't for the five-hundred-foot drop between the two Ragusas. But when the Vibram meets the road, every outing here is an adventure, even with my well-loved trail runners that grip the cobblestones like limpets.

The other day I went to buy breakfast at the nearby convenience store. Sicilian old cities, with cramped centers and nonexistent parking, haven't heard of Topps or Winn Dixie. These stores are no bigger than houses, and they're so cramped two shoppers can barely squeeze side by side, but they have everything you could want and more. The shelves bend under the weight of colorful vegetables and plump fruit that get weighed by the kilo. As I amble from one counter to the next, mesmerized by strange cuts of meat I never see at home, I get dizzy with the smell of cheeses.

They have almond cookies and crusty bread baked that morning and more inky Sicilian wines than I care to count — with an occasional Chianti thrown in for good measure. They have socks, umbrellas, sunscreen, and a wealth of things I don't recognize. But I digress again. We were talking about Ragusa.

Our place in Ragusa was a studio with a kitchen AND a garage. Steve got psyched when he heard about the garage since parking is a perpetual sore spot. But sadly, it was to stay that way. The garage, tucked under an old building on a one-way lane choking with scaffolding, wasn't sized for our Citroën AirCross SUV. So we parked in the street, as usual, and didn't move the car for three days, afraid of losing our parking spot. Walking up and down the Ragusan "streets" got us caught up with our cardio and allowed us to enjoy the excellent Sicilian hospitality without driving. And excellent it is. Some of our best meals in Sicily happened in Ragusa. *Ravioli* with wild boar? *Maccheroni* with hare? *Stinco de maiale*? My mouth still waters.

We eat out every day — sometimes for lunch, sometimes for dinner. Sicilian lunches are serious business. After a light breakfast of pastry and espresso — they call it a "*café normal*," though there's nothing normal about it, since it's strong enough to strip your teeth enamel — they're hungry by noon. So they spend a few sociable hours enjoying good food and company before succumbing to their siesta.

That's why everything but the restaurants is closed between noon and four: banks, shops, churches, hairdressers, doctor's offices — they're all out to lunch.

One of our most memorable lunches was at a cheese and wine shop across Portale San Giorgio, the only historical remnant of a church destroyed by the great earthquake. We stopped there because everything else was closed, and we were too cold and hungry to wait.

But this wasn't your typical Sicilian restaurant with *antipasti*, *primi*, and *secondi*. It wasn't even a pizzeria.

It was a modern, cozy, and light tasting experience. The red *Cerasuolo di Vittoria* was complex, smooth, and reasonable at 20 euros. The tasting menu of cheeses, caponata, *melanzana*, and sun-dried tomatoes, was generous and mouth-watering and went like a charm with the crusty, nutty bread. The warm ricotta I watched them make was comfort food at its best. Add the fresh *cannoli*, the exceptional service, and the views over Portale St. Giorgio, and you have one of those moments you'll never forget.

We took selfies with the owner, a charming young lady who hopes to see the U.S. someday. We exchanged emails and good wishes, hoping to meet again.

Happy with our lunch and new friend, we returned home, following a couple of *anziani* (elderly) who shuffled along, leaning on their walkers. They stopped to read the remembrance announcements plastered over the city walls: Filomena Varsano, 86. Giorgio Mercuria, 78. Emilio Centuri, 92.

They left, looking relieved.

"You think they're looking for their friends?" I asked.

Steve shook his head.

"More likely, they're looking to see if they're dead or not."

We said goodbye to Ragusa and headed toward Taormina with heavy hearts. It was like leaving an old friend. It had been home for only three days, but we'd miss it.

We drove away marveling at the green hills crisscrossed by tidy walls of round rocks. Some horizontal, turning the steep slopes into terraces for the vines; some almost vertical, ensuring that neighbors will never have to fight about their boundaries.

"This is not like America, where a rusty pin with a pink bow is all it takes to know what parcel belongs to whom, even a hundred years later," I said.

Steve, who taught me that, shook his head.

"Nothing here is like America."

30

ETNA AND TAORMINA

NOW LET ME CLARIFY: If you think Sicily is hot like I did, you're off the mark. The hottest I've been was in the shower, which didn't last long. These water heaters aren't built for Americans. You'd better have little to wash and be efficient about it. Otherwise, you'll end up much refreshed, as I did a few times. It's particularly unpleasant for the hair, though; thanks to my Parisian haircut, I don't have much left. Two months later, most fashion-minded folks would still call it "very short."

It may occasionally get warm enough to unzip your down hoodie, but not for long. That's why we got into sleeping with socks and long johns. Steve carries his Mechanix gloves in his pockets, and I always wear my cashmere sweater and scarf under my hi-tech raincoat, so I look like a bag lady, and I'm cool with that.

But Etna? That's in a different league.

The first hint was the sign stating that winter tires are required after November 15. But it was in Italian, so we ignored it. After all, we're coming from the North Country, so we know winter.

The next sign took it up a notch. Chains, they said.

We ignored that one too. It was a sunny bright day in mid-December with no snow in sight.

But for Etna's peak, of course. The higher we drove, the colder it got.

We stopped at a stand by the roadside to look for fruit. There was no fruit, but they had gloves, hats, and scarves. And, since my hands had gotten stiff with cold, that looked like a worthwhile investment.

I bought a pair of ugly gloves and a hat that made me look like Putin's grandmother, then we kept driving. White patches appeared, then expanded, until the only thing not white was the road. By the time we got to the Etna basecamp, the road was just a suspicion, and the air had turned into fog.

We parked in a snowbank and walked to see the lower craters. They're many, since Etna is not a monogamous volcano. The old witch unloads its ire through hundreds of tiny holes along the slopes, spewing fumes, ash, and sometimes more. But on this day, the fog was so thick we lost sight of the car before we left the parking lot.

We gave up and headed back. Pathetic, I know. I can't forgive myself. But I blamed it on my summer sneakers and Steve. What would he do if I fell in?

We headed down.

Fortunately, heading down didn't mean heading back. Like many other mountains, it turns out that Etna has more than one side. We'd seen the volcanoes of South Etna but not North Etna, where the wineries live. Etna's volcanic ash is just what wine needs, so the whole northern side of Etna is nothing but grapes.

I don't know about you, but if I had to choose between a freezing volcano shrouded in fog and a winery… Suffice it to say, we headed down, and Steve had a blast controlled-sliding the car down the hairpins. It turned out that our CrossAir was more of a summer car.

We left Etna, happy to have caught a glimpse of her splendor before the fog swallowed her, and started looking for a lunch place. Sadly, between Covid and winter, most restaurants were closed. We ended up at a local trattoria in Linguaglossa, one of Etna's hot wine destinations.

The food was excellent — *pasta con cinghiale* (wild boar,) *maccheroni* with wild hare ragout, followed by *stinco de maiale* — that's roasted pig leg, and it doesn't stink. The recommended local Etna Rosso was lovely too, and not cheap.

For entertainment, we watched the complicated machinations at the next table, figuring out who was who. We determined that the local commerce bureau was wining and dining a discerning lady with oversized round glasses. Chinese wine merchant, I thought, and I turned out to be correct. They all courted her and tripped all over each other to refill her glass with their best wines. She smiled, ate their food, enjoyed their wines, and then told them they were too expensive.

That was fun, but it was time to go.

I tried to signal the waiter, but he was busy eavesdropping too. I headed to the counter and waited politely as he chatted with another customer.

When the man left, I stepped forward to catch his eye, but he ignored me and took the bill to our table, where Steve was relaxing with his wine.

Really?

I got us the table. I ordered our food. I even complimented the wine, and now he treats me like I don't exist? I got mad.

Steve waved him back to me since I'm the one who pays. I did pay but didn't leave a tip, and I'm still angry.

Are you kidding me? Is this the twenty-first century?

Let me be clear: I do believe that men are equal to women,

and they deserve the same opportunities. I won't get angry when someone opens the door for me, pulls out my chair, or compliments me. I see it as a nod to a past when women were frail and men mattered. But this?

Three days later, I'm still smoking like Etna. But it is what it is. Nothing is perfect, not even Sicily.

As for us, we left Etna and headed down to Syracuse. Our home is the journey, remember?

31

SYRACUSE

SOMETHING BROKE on our way to Syracuse.

It was a lovely day with a toothsome sun, as we say in Romania. Everything looked bright and sunny, but we shivered like we were in withdrawal. We rushed down the highway heading toward Syracuse until we hit traffic. But we pushed through. We couldn't wait to find our new digs. The ads touted it as a lovely-looking apartment on the lovely island of Ortygia, the most historic place in Syracuse, the homeplace of guess who? Archimedes, of geometry fame.

That didn't do much for me. I've held a grudge against the dude ever since sixth-grade trigonometry. Still, I couldn't wait to see the place he ran naked out of his bathtub, excited about his findings. I just wished he'd done something about today's traffic.

Ortygia, an island connected to the mainland by two traffic-clogged bridges, was about as welcoming as a wasp's nest. Cars came at us from everywhere, and pedestrians crossed the busy roads like they owned them. Like really? Aren't roads made for cars?

Tired of following instructions, Steve — a rebel at heart —

turned right when Gwendolyn prompted him to turn left, so we got to drive all around Ortygia again. And again.

By the time we reached our reserved garage, we were too exhausted to care. We parked and dragged as many bags as we could to our new digs two blocks away.

The place was lovely — clean, pretty, well-organized, and tidy. But, like most places we've stayed in, it was windowless and freezing cold. The only pathetic heating contraption was a dehumidifier that needed draining every hour.

I rushed back to the garage to get our trusted heater, and we weathered the night. Still, the following morning I was too cold to get up.

When Steve woke up, he wasn't happy either. It had something to do with his socks. They'd somehow vanished in the shuffle, and he suspected me. Then he couldn't find the shampoo.

The dank cold room may have played a part — who knows? But a spark happened.

I'd had enough.

"How about going to Thailand? It's warm; we have a lovely place with windows and friends waiting for us."

Steve gave me a shattering look, but I don't shatter easily.

"This trip was lovely. It really was, for more than two months of it. But it's not warm, and it's not getting any better. If anything, it gets colder every day. We could do the rest of it next year. Spain, Portugal, whatever else. Let's do Italy, then head back to Paris and fly to Thailand."

Steve didn't like it. I knew he wouldn't. It's not just the food — he's not keen on Thai spices — but the language. He loves the friendly people but not the bureaucracy.

But we have more friends there than we have in the States. And it's warm.

Steve shrugged. "Let's."

32

LEAVING SICILY

WE LEFT Sicily for Reggio Calabria. That's the town sitting at the top of Italy's boot, but its only beautiful thing is the name. It's not that warm, either — the story of my life — but between wearing all our clothes, the space heater, and the wine, we'll make do, even though there's no food for miles.

That's flabbergasting. If there's one thing I learned about Italians — besides the fact that they speak with their hands — it is that they wouldn't get caught dead without fresh pasta, red wine, and fried fish. But not the ones here.

We walked for miles — 2½ to be precise — looking for a place to eat or buy food. We found zip. *Niente.* Nothing.

It's Monday after lunchtime — the witching time between 3 and 7 p.m. when restaurants are closed and the pizzerias haven't yet opened. It's December 20, one day short of the shortest day of the year, and the ghastly short days are haunted by cold winds looking for a place to warm up. The night starts before five, but there's no dinner till seven. And, like that's not bad enough, we had no lunch.

Thankfully, I have my emergency stash of peasant bread, cheese, salami, and olives. And wine, of course — after all, we're in Italy, where wine can get cheaper than water. But that's not what I signed up for. I want mouthwatering, steaming pasta and fragrant, hot pizza and wine. And I'm cranky.

It's been a long day. This morning, we said goodbye to Sicily. We recovered our car from the bowels of the Ortygia parking garage and headed North to Messina.

We'd planned on Christmas in Malta. We got ferry tickets, I found us a lovely apartment in Valetta, and I made reservations for Christmas Eve dinner. It was all going swimmingly until we heard the French news on Italian cable TV and discovered that Europe had another wave of Covid. France and Germany had closed their borders to Great Britain, the Netherlands had closed for a month before Christmas, and Israel red-listed France. That didn't bode well for our travels. Discovering that Italy required Covid testing to let us back from Malta was the clincher. This had started bad, and it would likely get worse. Getting stuck on the border looked likely, but it matters which side of it you're on. I can live getting stuck in France if Thailand keeps us out. Or in Italy, if France says no. But living in Malta until the pandemic disappears? No, thanks. I don't know much about Malta other than it's an expensive, Catholic island the size of a washcloth that thinks highly of itself. I can do three days to a week, but forever? Sign me out.

So we gave up the ferry tickets — 200 euros, but worth it, if you ask me — we canceled the lovely apartment, and forgot about Christmas dinner. We switched gears and headed to mainland Italy. We'd drive north to Messina, take the ferry across the straights to Reggio Calabria, and then drive to Basilicata and west to Puglia before heading north.

We packed our stuff, including our stash of food and wine collected from many splendid places. We checked that we didn't forget any chargers plugged in, emptied the fridge, and ensured the bleach was upright — another long story.

My heart was heavy.

I didn't miss the apartment — I got a little tired of old basements redecorated into fancy B&Bs with sexy neon lights and music in the double shower but no daylight, ever. I'm tired of being cold and dragging myself back to the car a mile away to recover Steve's socks or a forgotten phone charger.

I didn't miss Malta, either. I'm all for adventure, but lately, things have been a little tricky. Every time Steve looks at me crooked, I wonder if I'll need to carry him home. What home, you ask? Good question. So, heading toward home, whatever that may be, makes sense.

But I miss Sicily like I missed Corsica and Sardinia. Every time we leave to travel somewhere new, it breaks my heart to know we'll never be here again. Especially Sicily. Sicilians are lovely, the food is terrific, the wine doesn't suck, and the views are fantastic, provided you wear enough clothes. I'll miss Cefalu's beaches, Palermo's markets, Etna's snow, and Taormina's goat paths they call streets. I'll even miss Catania's fish market and the dark ashes falling from the sky, even though that was one of my least favorite places in Sicily.

I'll also miss our adventures. We're no longer young but still love to explore and enjoy life. We delight in nice dinners and good wine and laugh at things nobody else understands. Sure, we fight over the missing socks, the unread emails, and the parking — boy, do we fight over the parking. Still, at night we spoon in some rented hard bed with a hole in the middle deciding which side of the hole to sleep on.

Not for long now.

Whipped by the wind and the lashes of rain, I stand on the ferry deck and watch Sicily grow smaller and smaller, wishing I could carve it in my heart.

But I think it is.

33

REGGIO CALABRIA

No matter what Stanley Tucci, CNN's Italy expert, says, Calabria, the toe of the Italian boot poised to kick the living soul out of Sicily, is not the place to be. Reggio Calabria, its capital, is even less so. Hard to believe that it sits on the blue Mediterranean when you see its total lack of charm and the gray industrial apartment blocks that remind me of communism. Reggio is even worse than Catania, which was, until now, the only place in Italy I didn't like.

It has this beautiful name that rolls off your tongue like the name of good wine. *Corposo*, full-bodied, as Italian say it. But it doesn't deliver.

Our well-rated B&B had tall ceilings, a balcony, and a white marble bathroom. But the balcony looked over the neighbor's laundry and had no place to sit; the kitchen was bare: no corkscrew, no glasses, not even a plate. As for the soap and the shampoo, you wouldn't want your dog to smell like that.

Oh well. Some food and wine will help, we thought, so we went out for lunch. And we walked. And we walked.

For once, we happened to be out at the quintessential lunch hour — 1 to 2:30. We walked long dusty miles along garbage-sprinkled streets smelling like train toilets, but we found nothing to eat. Nothing but grungy houses and long rows of parked cars full of bored people waiting to pick up their kids.

When our feet refused to go any farther, we headed home. We dragged two chairs from the shared kitchen to our balcony, sat in the meager sun drinking our wine from coffee cups, and fought with the internet until the cold chased us in.

That's when we discovered that Thailand had closed its borders, thanks to the pandemic's new mutation. They may revisit things in January, but for now, our plans are on hold, and we're in limbo. We'll go back sometime, but in the meantime, we have to deal with the here and now. This Reggio Calabria stop was not one of my better moves. Time to go.

We canceled our second night in Reggio and drove to Matera, Basilicata's capital, which sits in Italy's instep.

The trip north was exhilarating. The highway runs along the Mediterranean, looking over the green hills covered with olive and orange trees, and dips in and out of tunnels before passing by the ancient Scylla. Homer's *Odyssey* calls it a six-headed monster who banded with her neighbor Charybdis to wreck every ship that ventured through the straights of Messina, but that's *passé*. Old Scylla has changed her wicked ways and turned into a lovely beach resort with an old castle by the sea. These days, the only thing she'll wreck is your wallet.

After Scylla, the highway heads north through the Apennines, Italy's mountainous spine. It crosses fields green even now in December, flies over tumultuous rivers, and skirts meadows so high that the sheep look like clouds.

Lovely trip, but, as always, things didn't go as planned. By the time we got lost in Scylla, got gas, which is always an adventure, and got turned around by the *carabinieri* for some inexplicable reason, it was time for lunch.

The first pizzeria was closed, of course. Pizzerias are

always closed for lunch. But a few miles later, we saw an open German restaurant.

German restaurant? In Italy? No offense to Germans; they are a great nation that excels in many fields, like discipline, cars, and beer. As for their humor and their cooking…

But we were just that hungry. So we stopped.

The place was empty but for one massive table hosting a family of ten, including two lively toddlers and an old gentleman so bent that I never saw his face.

We watched them shout amicably at each other as the owner built a fire of olive branches, took our order, and failed to interest us in appetizers.

He shrugged and returned with a basket of thick slices of delicious, crusty bread, a plate of Oregano-flavored black olives on the stone, and a bowl of something red and oily.

He grabbed my slice of bread — I wished he hadn't — spread some red concoction on it, and tried to feed it to me. Slightly miffed, I clenched my teeth and preempted by grabbing it myself. Boy, was it good! A fiery spread of red pepperoncini with olive oil, salt, and spices, strong enough to bring me to tears, burned my mouth into ashes.

Impressed with my delight, he returned with some *pattatini al'uovo* — an Italian version of scalloped potatoes. We inhaled them, so we were almost full before our pasta arrived.

I took a breather and glanced back at the family. The two well-worn women yelled at each other like they argued — but then here, everyone screams like they squabble. There are no hushed tones in Italy. Everything is loud, intense, and played in public for everyone to see.

One of the women got up to feed the dying fire. The old man turned to it to heat his hands. I got closer to the warmth and thanked her with two thumbs up.

"*Grazie*," she said.

"*No, Grazie a lei*," I said, and her coarse face melted into a smile.

We played peek-a-boo with the kids until the pasta came — *Salsiccia al Pomodoro* for Steve, hot sausage with tomato sauce, and *Gamberi e Nocciole* for me, shrimp with walnuts. They were scrumptious.

We left delighted, not only with the food but the owner's hospitality and the warmth of four generations of Italians sharing the pleasure of their lunch, the fire, and each other.

It melted my heart to see the old man showing the toddlers how to warm their hands to the fire — close, but not too close — and the tired women's smiles.

We drove on to Matera, famous for its *sassi* — cave-like ancient dwellings carved into the rock. Not long ago, Matera's *sassi* were just a bunch of unsanitary slums that the Italian government had to drag poor people out of. But these days, they're hot tourist attractions. They got converted into fashionable boutique shops, expensive restaurants, and fancy B&Bs.

We drove through another maze of narrow roads, stumbled upon another ZTL — *Zona Traffico Limitato* — and faced another parking headache. But, unlike Reggio's depressing gloom, Matera hops with restaurants, cafés, and bars. And they're open even now, at the witching hour between lunch and dinner. Everywhere you look, Christmas lights blink, decorations glitter, and smiling people bend under the weight of Christmas gifts. My kind of place!

Our new room is up a spiral ladder (I had fun dragging up the luggage), the internet is limping, and the bathroom is across the hallway. But we have glasses, a coffee maker, and even a corkscrew!

34

MATERA

MATERA, nestled in the high instep of the Italian boot, looks like a Nativity scene. That may be why it's a hot spot for movie makers, including Mel Gibson with his *Passion of the Christ*. The old buildings springing out of the honey-colored rock look warm in the sun, but they aren't. Still, unlike Reggio Calabria with its post-apocalyptic look, Matera hops with life. Gift-loaded people bump into each other on the narrow streets and smile. Bundled patrons loiter over coffee or *aperitivi*, people-watch, and chat, moving their hands a mile a minute.

It's the end of December and not warm. The midday sun has teeth, and the wind cuts through your layers, chilling your bones. My joints couldn't help but notice, so my days start with coffee, ibuprofen, and dreaming about warm places. The scarf I found months ago on Omaha Beach has been my faithful companion every day, though it's not something I'd ever buy. It's sprinkled with hot-pink grapefruits interspersed with electric-green kiwis in a garish pattern only a blind designer could concoct. But it's warm. Somewhere in Trapani, I found a neck warmer. I washed it and gave it to Steve. So, if you saw us and thought that half of our clothes were found in the street, you'd be right.

Steve rubs his hands to warm them, pulls on the Mechanix gloves he brought from home by mistake, and glares at the joyful patrons of an outdoor café.

"These people! How cold does it have to be to stop them from sitting outside?"

"There's no such thing. Sitting outside is what they do. It's a way of life."

And it is. Italians accept the weather for what it is and won't let it spoil their plans. Cold, rain, snow — whatever — they bundle up, grab their umbrellas, and go about whatever they're set to do. Every place we've been to has a lending bucket of umbrellas by the door. We were walking through Ragusa under torrential rain when a passerby suggested umbrellas. I tried, but it was a no-go. I could never get used to those cursed things. Half the time, they don't open; when they do, they act as sails and pull you with the wind that freezes your fingers on the handle. They hook you up with every stranger on the sidewalk before closing and dumping the water on your back. No thanks. I'll take a good raincoat any day.

Unlike Americans, who fight the cold with heaters and the heat with aircon, Italians shrug and move on. Winters are cold, so you dress for them or you shiver. Even inside. Most places we stayed at had no heating, and those that did wouldn't turn it on unless the temperature dipped below fifty. Same with summer. It's hot, so you wear loose clothing and hats. And you sweat.

I wish I had to worry about that now.

Cold or not, we regretted leaving Matera for Lecce, but the drive was a feast. As the ochre mountains gave way to plowed fields scattered between orange and olive groves, Matera's rock dwellings gave way to Puglia's idiosyncratic *trulli*.

What are *trulli*, you ask? They are a distinctive type of primitive dwellings, but they're built instead of carved. The classic ones are round, one-room structures with thick walls of piled rocks and conical roofs made of carefully layered flat stones to keep out the rain. The farmers and their animals sheltered under the same roof to keep each other warm. The *trulli* are said to keep out the winter's cold and the summer's heat. The light, too, I might add, since the windows aren't exactly a feature.

But that was long ago. These days, the *trulli* are a hot commodity. Italian and foreign investors scooped them up and restored them into ubiquitous B&Bs and vacation homes. And, since modern people need more space, they broke holes in the walls to add another *trullo*, then another, making them into luxurious clusters.

We stopped to explore them. Steve wondered about the prices, and I wondered what life would be like if we lived here. What would we do once we finish restoring it? Read? Garden? Then what?

I can read with the best of them, but my gardening is pathetic, and my wanderlust is all-consuming. I go nuts if I don't have things to see, do, and learn. And so does everyone around me. So we moved on.

It was lunchtime, but, as always, places to eat were few and far between. Most restaurants were closed even when Mr. Google said they were open. Still, lucky us, we found an open *locanda*. We snagged a parking space and rushed in.

The vast room was cold and eerily empty, like the aftermath of an alien kidnapping. Heavy wood tables sported white tablecloths, Christmas music hummed from the speakers, and glitzy decorations fluttered in the draft. Still, there was nary a soul in sight.

"Hello!" I hollered.

I heard something scurry in the kitchen, and a plump woman appeared.

"*Si?*"

"*Due? Per mangiare?*" Two? To eat?

She stared at us with wide eyes.

"Now?"

I checked my watch. 1:10 p.m. The perfect time for Italian lunch. Or so I thought.

"*Si.*"

"OK. Pick a table."

We did, without much hope. Her question didn't inspire confidence.

She wiped off the laminated menus. The house wine, a "*Vino Amabile,*" at 5 euros for a half-liter carafe; four to five starters, and just as many *primi* and *secondi*.

Steve shrugged.

"They won't have all this."

That's not uncommon. Pizza for lunch is a rarity, even if it is on the menu, and two-thirds of the listed things are unavailable. That's why we always have a plan A and a plan B.

I settled for the *Ciccieti ala Zucco de Cinghiale con fungi,* homemade pasta with mushrooms and wild boar sauce, and the *Trippa de Vitello alla Suggo de Pomodoro*, veal tripe with tomato sauce. Steve chose the *Polpette al Sugo*, meatballs in tomato sauce.

We kept in reserve the *Linguini al Sugo de Asino* — the linguini with mule sauce — and the horse steak.

We ordered. The woman nodded.

"You have all this?" Steve asked.

She looked at him like he'd grown a third ear.

"Of course."

And she did.

The food was scrumptious. The *polpetti* were tiny flavor

bombs smothered in luscious tomato sauce. The *trippa*, cooked with a hint of spice and garlic, melted in your mouth. The pasta was mouth-watering and al dente, but not too much, though it arrived after the *secondi*. Then our new friend Josie brought us — on the house — some sweets with almonds and honey and two flutes of the best *granitas* I've ever had. They were slushies made with berries, almonds, and a touch of grappa. That was one of the best meals we've had throughout our travels. I still drool when thinking of it.

Just as we lamented that nobody else partook of the deliciousness, a party of ten showed up carrying a giant birthday cake, and the place came alive.

Once again, in Italy, things are not what they seem. Sit tight and watch them happen.

35

CHRISTMAS IN LECCE

LIFE WORKS IN STRANGE WAYS.

For the last week or so, things have been getting to us. It's late December, and we're tired of cold, dark, cramped apartments with lousy internet and Italian-only news on TV. Sick of wearing the same clothes, not too clean at that, for the last two months. Fed up with lugging our ever-expanding luggage — half of it food and a quarter space heater — from parking spaces a mile away. We want a place to be warm and cozy, with our old books lying open on the side table, our slippers by the sofa, and Paxil purring in our lap. We want to be home.

But we can't.

Thanks to Omicron raising its ugly head, we canceled our trip to Malta and a darn good-looking Christmas dinner. Then Thailand closed, putting an end to our trip to the sun.

The rich food and abundant wine requiring my daily attention shrunk my pants, while Steve got so skinny that I'm afraid a gust of wind will whisk him away.

We miss Guinness, Paxil, and our son. We even miss Christmas shopping — we can't buy anything because we can't carry it.

All in all, a rather gloomy picture. We felt cranky and sorry for ourselves as we drove from Matera to Lecce.

"Where are we staying tonight?" Steve asked, dreading another folded-mirrors adventure.

"I dunno. I checked so many places I forgot what I ended up booking. I just know we can't check in before 2, and we can't drive in before 4. The streets are closed."

"What?"

"They messaged me that the place is in the ZTL. We can't get in before 4."

Steve cut his eyes to me as a heavy truck barged toward us.

"What?"

"ZTL. *Zona Traffico Limitata.* That's the town center. Inbound traffic is only allowed from 4 to 7. If we get there sooner, we have to park elsewhere."

Steve shook his head and drove on, narrowly avoiding a couple of pedestrians and a black cat on a suicide mission. I looked around for more cats when I saw a sign: *Produse Românești*, Romanian products. That gave me an idea.

"Can you stop?"

Stopping Steve is not easy. Nor is getting him going. For some inexplicable reason, Steve's inertia doesn't obey the laws of physics that say that inertia is a function of mass. Steve's mass has steadily diminished while his inertia has increased exponentially with age. So it took him a quarter of a mile to ask, "Why?"

"There's a Romanian store. I want to get some stuff for Christmas."

Another quarter mile, and he stopped. I ran to the store and raided it of everything that looked Christmasy and some things that didn't.

"I got stuff! I got *sarmale*, and *mici*, and *costiță*, and *țuică*."

I even got a can of *Ciucaș*, Steve's favorite Romanian lager, brewed in Brasov, my Transylvanian hometown. Steve says *Ciucaș* is excellent, and I know it's the water. Brasov's water is hard and colder than water should be in its liquid form since it comes from the Carpathians. It surely can't be the hops since Transylvania is not known for its hops. It has pine forests, thirsty vampires, and alpine meadows. Hops? Not so much. But I digress again.

Steve looked mildly pleased and massively skeptical.

"Do you have a kitchen?"

Do we have a kitchen? Good question. Maybe? But even if we do, that doesn't mean much. The last one had no pots, pans, or cutlery. We ate our breakfast croissants off paper napkins, which is the norm in Italy. But I couldn't cook a Romanian Christmas dinner on paper napkins. I needed a stove, pots and pans, and preferably an oven.

Oh well. Too late to worry. We pushed on.

We reached the ZTL two minutes before four. We stopped, pretending to check the map until the *carabinieri* moved past us, then drove the narrow streets choking with festive pedestrians carrying Christmas gifts. They gave us distinctly un-Christian glares. One even showed the *carabinieri* his watch and pointed to us. The *carabinieri* told him to put on his mask, which must be Italian for "stuff it."

We meandered through a maze of narrow lanes at sub-pedestrian speed until we found our street, but the turn was too steep to negotiate. So I walked to look for a place to park while Steve held on strong against the drivers blowing their horns and making hand gestures remotely related to Nativity.

Wonder of wonders, there was a place to park. Our door opened to a palatial apartment, the best we've had throughout our trip. Two massive rooms full of light, tall ceilings with stone arches, glimmering floors, a dining table crowned with a marbled cake, a private patio with chairs, and beautiful stone stairs.

Steve's jaw dropped.

"Is all this ours?"

"I hope so."

"Where are the stairs going?"

I shrugged. I just hoped they weren't going to the bathroom — you'll figure out why as you age.

But no. The bathroom was just a quarter-mile away, off the hallway, off the bedroom, off the living room.

"So then, what's up there?"

It turns out that "up there" was a second tiny bedroom and the kitchen. Not much of it — a sink and a two-plate induction stove but no fridge, microwave, or oven. Still, better than paper napkins.

So I set up to cook us a Romanian Christmas dinner.

If you don't know it — and I bet you don't — a Romanian Christmas dinner is an elaborate affair that takes weeks to plan, days to cook, and hours to eat. It comprises a variety of heavy appetizers, then *sarmale (*stuffed pickled cabbage), fried meats, and sausages served with *mămăligă* (polenta) and washed down with wine. It ends with *cozonac* — a Romanian *pannetone* filled with walnuts, poppy seeds, and raisins — and cake, preferably chocolate.

I didn't have that. But I could put together the *sarmale*, some *mici* — fluffy Romanian skinless sausages grilled and served with mustard — and *cozonac*.

I got cooking, but the challenges wouldn't quit.

Turning on the induction stove required a genius. Lucky for me, I had one handy — who else would have married me? Steve got it going.

The pots were pasta pots; therefore, they had holey lids to let out the steam, and that's a no-no for *sarmale*. There was no cutting board, so I julienned the pickled cabbage on the dish-dripping tray. There was no oil. But I remembered a condiment package of olive oil I had absconded from someplace, so I turned the car upside down and found it.

There was no cooking knife. But our trusty Opinel knife/corkscrew proved helpful again.

Did you know that pickled cabbage can find every scratch on your hands and set it on fire? Neither did I, but I found out.

Fast forward two hours, and this Italian palatial apartment smells like my childhood home, but for the garlic. In Romania, you don't put garlic in *sarmale*. It keeps away the vampires, so none of your relatives could come for dinner. But all I had to flavor my *sarmale* was the *Pasta Mafioso* spice mixture I'd bought in Palermo. The oregano, pepper, basil, and sun-dried tomatoes were OK, but the slivers of dried garlic would be anathema in Transylvania. But that's far away.

I set my gifts for Steve under the Christmas decoration hanging on the door. A bottle of red Salento waits to be opened. The *mici* are waiting for the grill, but they have a long wait. There's no grill, so I'll just fry them in the pan.

Steve has been a good sport about this, but I know he's worried. As we finished breakfast, he asked what we'd do about lunch.

I told him we'd have lupper — lunch and supper — around two.

He sighed.

Minutes later, he asked if there was anything else to eat besides *sarmale*. I told him about the *mici*. He nodded, but I could tell he was worried. He never asks about food, and he's never hungry. He forgets to eat unless I feed him. I wish I had that problem! But I can see he's on edge.

To compensate for what may be another Christmas disaster, I made reservations to an excellent place for tomorrow. But

Steve misses his turkey, his ham, the apple pie, and our friends. I do too.

But we'll have the best Romanian Christmas I can put together for now. And, to get in the mood, we'll start with that Salento.

36

LECCE

IT TURNS out that the *Leone de Castris Salice Salento* is dark purple, voluptuous, and smooth. It tastes like blackberries and *amarena* — bitter cherry — with a hint of basil reminding you that you're in Italy. It goes down like a fiend.

It also turns out that the Romanian shopkeepers know their job and like their food, so everything I bought was first class.

I started cooking the *mici* in a pan, turning them over every 15 seconds until Steve could no longer watch. He took over. I was wary at first — who wouldn't be? His knowledge of all things Romanian doesn't go beyond four-letter words. But he cooked them better than I ever could. They were steamy and juicy with a dark golden crust and a flavor that made your mouth water. We dipped them in Dijon mustard and ate them on thick crusty bread. We were no longer hungry by the time they were done, so the *sarmale* lived to see another day.

We opened our gifts. Steve got two T-shirts and a bottle of aged grappa — distilled grape liquor, Italy's answer to bourbon, gin, and vodka. I got a bottle of pepperoncini-flavored olive oil and a box of three-quarter Italian fashion socks in colors I had never dreamed I'd wear.

After dinner, we joined the *passeggiata*, like everyone else in Lecce. That's when every Italian walks the streets with their loved ones to see and be seen. Elderly grannies leaned on their walkers while young fashionistas limped on their ten-inch high-heels, struggling to hold on to their toddlers. Dogs showed off their new long-sleeved hoodies. Everyone walked in a ritualized dance, showing off their latest fashions, their new boyfriend, their new toy. Christmas lights brought magic to the old dark streets, and street musicians filled the air with harmony, from Christmas music to Bach. Dogs barked, kids screamed, women laughed, and lovers whispered in each other's ears in the low, hushed tones of foreplay.

The night air was heavy with the scent of Christmas wreaths, the mouth-watering aroma of grilled meat, and the smoke of cigars mingling with expensive perfume.

People took pictures of the enormous Nativity scene by the Roman amphitheater without realizing they were the show. Italians, with their intensity, curiosity, and love of all good things in life. They, and Lecce.

I didn't expect to like Lecce. Everything I'd read about it said that it's an over-ornate, self-impressed city with overdone baroque buildings and over-the-top churches. I guess the one word that describes Lecce is "over."

But, as we rambled through the narrow streets, breathing its scents through our masks, listening to its music, and relishing the street show, Lecce was magic. The ornate honey-colored buildings looked charming in the moonlight, with their elaborate decorations half-hidden by the shadows. We wondered about the performances this old Roman amphitheater hosted two thousand years ago. We clomped about the cobblestones, admiring the multitude of Christmas gifts displayed in store windows and listening to laughing people shout words we couldn't understand. But we got their passion for life and were glad to be there, walking hand in hand.

37

HEADING NORTH

CHRISTMAS IS OVER, and so is Lecce. And with it, so is the southern tip of Italy, that high heel mostly unknown to tourists, therefore authentic and affordable.

I had a little heartbreak leaving our palatial place in Lecce — it was beautiful, spacious, in the middle of things, and even warm, for God's sake.

But, as Romanians say, "*Calatorului ii sta bine cu drumul*" — the traveler looks better on the road. So we packed the clothes we'd washed in the sink and fast-dried on the heaters, and I bagged the *sarmale*. We grabbed the couple of — OK, OK, it was six — bottles of ridiculously cheap Salento wine I'd acquired at the supermarket and headed out.

We squeezed out through the narrow streets, avoiding the disapproving glares of the stone Caryatids poxed with acid rain holding up the heavy roofs, and headed South. We couldn't head north before reaching the tip of the heel. So we did.

Santa Maria de Leuce, the tip of the heel, is supposed to be a lively resort town, but it was eerily quiet on Christmas morning. The blue sea was busy sparkling, but people had better things to do than clutter the streets. We took a few pictures, then headed North toward Sorrento, hugging the steep cliff about to crumble into the blue Mediterranean. We coveted every single one of the sun-drenched villas overlooking the sea that soaked up the morning sun, wondering what living there would be like. Coffee on the patio? Writing under the midday sun? Wine at sunset? It sounded better than any place we'd ever lived. That heel's beauty fills your heart.

But sadly, one needs more than beauty to live on. So we dragged ourselves north, hugging the cliff at every hairpin turn, struggling to stay with the traffic. But, as usual, we got lost.

We U-turned on a side road behind a stopped car. It merged onto the main road, despite the deafening roar of a motorcycle zipping by. The crash almost happened, but the bike swerved dangerously close to the cliff and barely made it. The motorcyclist lifted his hand in a finger salute and pushed on.

The car froze.

We waited for it to move on, but it didn't. After what felt like a week, it changed direction and headed south. We shrugged and headed north, wondering why they'd changed their mind until we found the motorcyclist and his friends waiting for them half a mile up the road. The car must have known it, so they changed direction, even though that was the only road for miles and miles.

Having learned what to do if we cut someone off, we pushed north and switched west.

If you're like me, you imagine Italy as a fancy high-heeled boot sticking south into the Mediterranean, ready to kick Sicily like it's a turd in its way. Am I right?

But, like me, you'd be wrong. Italy is not north-south; it's oblique. It goes from northwest to southeast. So what, you ask?

Going straight north, you'll end up in the water. To go north, you need to head west, so our east-west crossing turned out to be a trip northwest. But I bet you don't care, so let's forget about it and call it heading west. But the older-than-dirt Apennines that make Italy's spine get in the way, so there's no straight path. For miles and miles, there's nothing but hairpin turns, majestic views, and merry Christmasy drivers sitting on their horns congratulating each other for their driving.

Inventive as ever, Steve took a few shortcuts to nowhere and bought us a couple extra hours of driving on top of the full day we had planned. We were tired when we got to Sorrento. Like really tired.

"Where's this place? And what is it?" Steve asked, with that twitch by his jaw that tells me he's had it.

I'd had it too. Besides Gwendolyn, the navigator, nobody gets blamed more often than me. Whether it's goats on the road, construction delays, or lousy weather, it's always my fault. And let me tell you: If I could order better weather, I would. I'd even pay for it, for God's sake, but no one offered.

I took a deep breath.

"It's in Sorrento. It's a small bungalow inside a lemon grove between a motorcycle dealership and a gas station."

Steve snorted.

"Of course. A lemon grove. In the heart of Sorrento. Why not? I can see that happening. So where's this magical place?"

I gave him directions, but truth be told, I was wary. I'd spent hours with Mr. Google, trying to pin down this place that looked just as likely as a stable full of unicorns.

Our nerves were frayed by the time we saw the sign for Paradise Garden. It was, as expected, between the gas station and the motorcycle dealership. But the gate was locked.

I rang the doorbell. Nothing happened. I turned my back on the smoke coming from Steve's ears and called the owner. No one answered. I tried again.

I was considering running away, hoping I was faster than

Steve when a car stopped next to us. The smiling owner apologized for being late and opened the gates.

My jaw fell. That place was everything we hoped for and more, even though the part about the lemon grove was a lie. It wasn't just lemons. It had lemons, oranges, walnuts, and some bizarre yellow citrus as big as a football they call *cedre*. Delicious with a sprinkle of sugar.

That place was the dreamiest place I can remember, and it had everything we hoped for, from parking and heat to a microwave.

I couldn't resist.

"I guess it was in a lemon orchard, after all."

Steve rolled his eyes.

"I guess so."

38

CAPRI

THANKS TO AXEL MUNTHE'S magic *The Story of San Michele*, I've dreamed about Capri since I was a child. Despite my mother's watchful eyes, my reading was quite eclectic. I read everything I could find, from femme-fatale biographies and hard-boiled mysteries to the health book that explained how children occurred, but bypassed the stork. I spent every spare moment reading until my mother found the remedy: She lit a bonfire and burned all my books.

The horrid things Tiberius did to young people? The fisherman he killed by having his minions rub a poisonous fish in his face? The orgies? I was all in. I couldn't wait to see the island of Capri, where it had all happened.

Cruising from Sorrento to Capri is a piece of cake. Sorrento's port was downtown, just a mile away and a few hundred rough steps down. We'll buy a ferry ticket, and we'll be on our way, I thought.

Not so fast, Sparky!

"You need the FF2 masks," the ferry woman said.

I pointed to the two-ply quilted mask I was wearing.

"Like this?"

She shook her head so hard I was glad it didn't come off.

"No, no. FF2." She showed us a picture of something we know as KN95.

We have a few of those — how could we not, in these Covid-cursed times? But they're a mile away, in the car, and we're here.

I gathered my credit card and looked around for Steve, who was MIA, like every time I got myself in trouble. The Capri trip was a goner. Tomorrow, maybe. If I could talk Steve into it. But it was December 31st, the eve of the Capo D'Anno — New Year — and half a holiday. My Capri dream was turning to smoke.

"They have them for sale at the Info Office. Right there."

The woman pointed to a door fifty feet away. "But hurry. The ferry leaves soon."

"Thanks."

I headed to the Information Office with the speed of desperation. The three *anziani*, the old folks inside, were watching a soccer rerun. They stared at me stumbling in.

"*Due masquerine, prego?*" I mumbled.

They stared at each other in astonishment. I guess my twenty-five years of U.S. living didn't help my Italian accent.

"*DUE. MASQUERINE.* For the ferry," I yelled and covered my mouth and nose to demonstrate.

The hands got moving. They started debating in an Italian too quick for me to follow. My request was apparently highly unusual, though the sign posted on the door: "*FF2 Masquerine, 4 Euro,*" said otherwise.

The white-haired guy looking like Santa grabbed a box and showed it to the important-looking guy at the desk. He nodded.

Santa took out two black KN95 wannabes wrapped in cellophane and handed them to me. Suffused with gratitude, I offered him my credit card.

"*Grazie.*"

He stepped back like I'd offered him a snake.

More gestures and raised voices, too fast for me to follow, other than the word "*carte,*" card. I held up my VISA, hoping someone would take it. They didn't.

The man at the desk said something, then put his hands in his pockets. I was cooked.

Santa nodded.

"Sorry, we no take VISA. But take them. Free for you."

"Free? I just take them and go?"

"Yes. Free. Just for you."

I thanked them profusely and scrambled back to the ticket booths, showing the woman my masks.

"Good," she said, processing my card and handing me two tickets. "Now, run to *posto* 4."

"Run?"

"Run."

Run we did to get a better spot in line behind a hundred other travelers. As we waited, a smooth-talking gentleman offered us a boat ride around Capri. Eighteen euros only to see everything that mattered: Grotta Azzura, Tiberio's villa, and much more. Boy, was I tempted, but I decided that flexibility was worth more than a questionable discount. I regretfully declined.

We shuffled in, looking for a space to breathe. Not many. The forward seats, the only ones with a bit of a view, were all taken, so we settled on two midship seats offering a spectacular view of the seats ahead. But at least we were in.

The speakers started screaming.

"The seas are rough. Move to the back if you have a delicate stomach."

We both have delicate stomachs. But, being who we are, we

moved forward toward the view as wiser travelers moved to the back.

They weren't lying. The seas were so rough they threw us in the air. We held on to the seats and fell back until my stomach decided to divorce its breakfast. I wondered if I should sacrifice my hat when the ferry people started distributing plastic shopping bags. We weren't into shopping, but puking was high on our list, so I grabbed two. Bags in our hands, we kept falling in and out of the long, slow waves, wishing we'd stayed home. Our stomachs followed slowly. But we made it to Capri, and, a bit worse for the wear, we stumbled out behind the other unfortunate travelers.

We watched a dozen ill-looking folks shuffle to join the boat ride around the island. Steve sighed with relief.

"Aren't you glad we aren't going?" he asked.

"Are you kidding? I don't want to ever set foot in another boat. I can't even think about heading back!"

Steve nodded.

"And to think I always wanted a sailboat," he said.

We sat on the curb and waited for our stomachs to settle before exploring the island. Sadly, after all that struggle, Capri turned out to be a disappointment.

Gone are Axel Munthe's steep goat paths edged by silver-green olive trees. They've been replaced by narrow roads choking with tourists shopping for trinkets and stinky old cars blowing their horns to curse at each other. Walking to Anacapri to see San Michele proved impossible. There were no sidewalks along the roads too narrow for two cars abreast. And after that boat trip, stuffing ourselves in a crowded bus was unthinkable.

Still, after fifty years of longing, I couldn't give up on Capri without at least one good memory. So, like I always do, I followed the locals.

They're easy to recognize even in the most tourist-spoiled

places. They don't take pictures, don't buy trinkets, and don't crowd the overpriced downside cafés. They seldom drink in the morning and don't shout at each other in English.

They drag shopping carts and buy groceries. They walk their dogs slowly but with purpose along the least traveled alleys and stop to chat with the shopkeepers. They're stooped little ladies wearing three-quarter socks and white-haired gentlemen leaning on sculpted canes that measure you with wary eyes.

So follow them we did, up roads too narrow for vehicles to tackle. We climbed further and further until the sunny streets emptied, leaving us alone with the pigeons soaring above the glittering blue sea. We followed the wind and chased the leaves until we found Axel Munthe's Capri. The Natural Arch, a graceful rock formation sculpted by the wind and shaped by the rain, guarded the uncanny blue sea.

We sat on a stone bench, reflecting on how things change, and still, they stay the same. We took a ton of pictures, like the tourists we are, then headed back.

My heart was full.

But my throat was sore, and my head ached. I feared I'd gotten Covid.

39

NEW YEAR 2022

I DON'T KNOW about you, but my 2021 was terrible, horrible, lousy, and just no good. It came with so much hope — how hard could it be to best 2020? Just get rid of that darn Covid, will you, and everything else is gravy. I'll take lousy weather, high prices, and even bad luck as long as the pandemic is over. Wouldn't you?

But 2021 failed worse than I thought it could. The pandemic continued. So did the political rage dividing friends and families. We sold our lovely house on the lake and moved into a tiny cabin in the woods, planning to spend the winter in Thailand. We lived like bums, imposing on our son and friends to do our laundry and ditch the trash. It may sound funny, but it's not. Believe it or not, crashing with people when you're seventy is not as cool as when you're seventeen.

But, come winter, we couldn't go to Thailand thanks to Covid. We settled for driving Southern Europe, which sounds far more glamorous than it is. Three months into our trip, we're moving from place to place every other night. Some have heat, some parking, some Wi-Fi, and some none of the above. It got old. We're ready to bury 2021 in Sorrento on Italy's Amalfi coast.

Our tiny bungalow — kitchen, living, and bedroom all in one — has no Wi-Fi to speak of. Still, it has heat, a stovetop, and even a microwave. And it sits in a marvelous citrus orchard.

When I booked it, I feared it was fake. Many are. The free parking turns out to be half a mile away in the street. The included breakfast turns out to be crackers with a bottle of eternal milk. The beds are hard as rocks, and the showers temperamental. And don't even get me started on the pillows! For a neck pain specialist like me, there's nothing more important than the pillow — unless the bathroom is on a different floor.

But this time, it was real. The orange trees, heavy with oranges; the lemon trees, rich with flavor; the partitions made of rosemary bushes — all real. And all ours for a few days.

Can't think of a better place to celebrate the new year. I booked a nice place to have dinner, and we went to Capri.

Then Covid hit.

I'm not sure it's Covid since I didn't get tested. But I've got a sore throat, a swollen head, chills, and aches from my teeth to my toes, so I know it's a virus. And I've been isolating like Robinson Crusoe and masking like a bank robber. What else could I get?

Then Steve started. Fatigue, burning eyes, malaise, and no joy in life.

Now what?

We're in a foreign country where we don't know anyone. I can't even call 911 since I don't know its Italian equivalent. We can't really self-isolate since we have no food and no medications. And we're leaving tomorrow to God knows where.

I did the best I could.

I booked an extra night in the orchard. We put on our FF2 masks, bought some food, then locked the door and turned the TV on to France 24 since there's nothing in English, and my French is way better than my Italian.

I picked lemons and rosemary from the garden and made tomato-basil bruschetta and lemon chicken with rosemary and rice. Then, exhausted, we packed it in at 4 p.m.

It's still 2021, darn it, for another eight hours. But then it's over, and 2022 will come bringing new hope. Isn't it time for some joy?

My hopes for '22 are modest. For us to stay alive, not too damaged by the ruthlessness of time. Safety and health for our son and our friends. And hopefully, new beginnings for us all. Is it too much to ask?

Thunderous fireworks woke us at midnight. We watched the shower of light and color exploding behind the olive trees, so many that the air turned to smoke. It made me smile, though my throat burned, my head ached, and Betty White had just died. Shame on you, lousy year! Couldn't you just leave her alone?

Good riddance, '21. Welcome, '22.

40

FALLING ON VESUVIUS

WE LOVED SORRENTO, despite winter, Covid, isolation, and all. Leaving it was hard. As a matter of fact, it was hard to leave every place other than Catania and Reggio Calabria. I loved them all. I loved the people, the food, the wines, and the excitement of the new places. I loved dreaming about a possible life as a local everywhere we stayed, from Corsica's wild Bastia to Sardinia's seductive Cagliari, Palermo's throbbing markets, Taormina's entangled stairs, Lecce's charm to Sorrento's elegance. Leaving gave me heartache every time since I knew we wouldn't be back. All those alternative lives in which I woke up in a tiny apartment, walked out to get fresh pastries, and then sat on the balcony to gossip with the neighbors were just dreams. But they were beautiful while they lasted.

We left Sorrento's lemon grove to head north. We'll stop to say hi to Vesuvius, then continue north to our next temporary home. It's an *agriturismo* in Dolgio, a village too small to fit on the almost life-size map I'd bought at Feltrinelli, Italy's most famous bookstore. And, as always, we don't know what we'll find. Will we have heat? Wi-Fi? Hot water? Parking, however, should be a breeze since it's a farm and there's nothing else for miles.

We skipped Pompeii since we'd seen it before, but you shouldn't. It's worth it — the ruins, the ceramics, the pained bodies preserved in the ashes, the bordello's visual menu, the roads just wide enough for one chariot with stepping stones across so you don't get your feet wet.

The day was overcast, with clouds so low they looked like fog. But once we climbed high enough to break through, the morning sun bathed us in its glorious glow. The surrounding mountains peaked through the clouds like dark islands in a sea of snow. It made for good pictures, though not great views. We circled the grungy crater, dodged the sellers of all things kitsch from miniature volcanoes to painted plates and plastic fans, and headed back down.

We skipped the crowded shuttle to walk the mile to the car. A piece of cake. Unless you look the wrong way.

I was eavesdropping on some noisy birds' heated exchange when I stepped into a hole. My left ankle twisted and gave. I plunged forward on my knees and stayed there a while.

Steve helped me up, and I assessed the damage.

The left ankle hurt, but the right knee felt funny. It didn't hurt, but it got wet and sticky. I pulled up my pants to view the damage. Not good.

After cleaning some of the blood, I found a deep one-inch-long bleeding laceration and a dozen scratches on the leg. No big deal. The problem was the three-inch, L-shaped laceration on top of my knee, where the skin hung loose. I needed stitches. Or staples. No glue would fix that.

But I had no stitches and no staples. No antibiotic cream, no alcohol, no hydrogen peroxide, no bandages, no nothing. It's 2 p.m. on a Sunday, and we're on top of a volcano, heading to some place four hours away that we know nothing about.

What would you do?

Go to the hospital? Of course. That's what any reasonable person would do. Not me. I'm a retired ER doc, and I know what the ER will be like on Sunday evening in Covid times. No can do.

Time to get creative.

I got the grappa from the trunk — a 40-percent alcohol grape distillate. Not quite rubbing alcohol, but better than nothing. I cleaned the wounds with grappa-soaked toilet paper. It didn't feel good, but in the indomitable spirit of old Westerns, I'd use some internally for anesthesia.

I stuck toilet paper to the wounds and held pressure to stop the bleeding, and we drove on.

We headed north, keeping our eyes peeled for a pharmacy, but we had no luck. So I made do. I bought a roll of duct tape at a gas station, and Steve cut it into strips with his Swiss Army knife scissors. I stretched the loose skin over the wound to close the gap and taped it back in place.

It had been dark for hours when we finally got to our *agriturismo* in the woods. Our host, young Leonardo, showed us the tiny apartment between the vines, but it was too dark to see anything but the bed. And the giant black scorpion in the bathroom.

I asked Leonardo for some antibiotic ointment and a bandage. He returned with a first aid kit and a broom to evacuate our roommate, but the scorpion was already gone.

I took a hot shower, washed the damaged knee with soap and hot water, then doused it in honey. If you ever get hurt on top of some volcano, don't forget that the honey is hyperosmolar and bactericidal. That's why it works as well as antibiotic ointments, but it tastes much better. I retaped the gash, wrapped it in a bandage, and went to bed.

If this works, I'm an even better doctor than I thought.

41

WHINING A LITTLE

Our *AGRITURISMO*, *Borgo Struginato*, is a wild mish-mash of stone buildings, garages, chicken coops, and dog pens at the bottom of a green hill covered in olive trees and vines. The main building is stately and dignified. Judging by its skinny bell tower sheltering a silent bell, it must have started life as a church. But it rubs shoulders with a plastic kids' gym, a row of horse stalls inhabited by chatty red chickens, and a December vegetable garden light on charm and heavy on cabbage, anise, and broccoli. The star of the garden is the kale, with its fleshy dark green leaves patterned like dinosaurs' skin and just as edible.

The guard dog, Spritz, is a handsome Maremma sheepdog. That's an Umbrian shepherd breed, so white and wooly you could easily mistake him for a sheep. He jumps on you, plops over to get scratched, and is always ready to play. His partner, whose name seems to be "the truffle dog," is a neurotic brown pointer always locked in her pen.

Besides the dogs and the red chickens, there's a variety of wild birds, bugs, spiders, plus the black scorpion that welcomed us. I've been checking my shoes for him ever since.

Leonardo is a mechanical engineer. He goes to work every day while his friendly parents, who don't speak English, putter around the farm from daybreak to dark. Dressed in a sock-style hat hiding her short dark hair and a grungy padded coat that has seen better days, Maria spends her days with the wheelbarrow. She pushes it up the hill to gather the olive trimmings they use as kindling, then does her best to hold it back on the way down. Her husband, Antonio, is round-faced and flushed and has an inordinate affection for the eight-foot ladder he carries with him everywhere.

They stopped by with gifts. Maria brought store-bought turkey breast and cheesy breadsticks, while Antonio brought some wine of his own production. They don't look much younger than us, but their retirement isn't in the cards. Just watching them makes me tired.

Our tiny apartment has a bedroom that overlooks the vines, a bathroom with a shower (and a bidet, of course), and a kitchen with an impressive fireplace. It's almost warm, cozy, and comfortable, but for the paucity of sitting places. You can choose between the kitchen chair, the bed, and the toilet. I have yet to try the bidet.

There's no TV, but the internet works well enough to stream BBC. The pool between the olive trees must be lovely in summer. But now, when the sun sets at 4:30, and a lively wind chases heavy clouds across the sky and whips them into rain every now and then, I'd trade that pool for a hot shower.

I couldn't hope for a better place to shelter, and I'm grateful to be here. But not happy.

This year has started poorly. My sore throat turned into a wet, heavy cough that robs me of my sleep. Two days later, the darn knee's still bleeding, despite copious amounts of honey and duct tape. And the incessant rain turned the farm into a mud bath only a dog could love.

Then I'm upset about Thailand. My plans to head there fell apart. They froze their test-and-go program, so the only way in is through a week-long isolation, and they're not kidding: No outside privileges, no take-out food, no alcohol, not even Motrin or Tylenol in case they masked a fever.

No can do.

I canceled the lovely room in Bangkok with its jacuzzi and the five days in Paris. Steve is working on getting back the money for the flights.

For now, we'll continue to Genoa, cross into France, and head west toward the Basque country, then cross into Spain and DRIVE the Camino to Santiago de Compostela. Though you never know. I may walk some of it while Steve snoozes. Then Portugal, back into Spain, then a couple of weeks near Alicante. Who knows? It is what it is, and it could be worse.

But I was ready for Thailand, staying put in one place, and some semblance of normalcy. I hoped to be warm, sleep in my own bed, and get back into shape — you wouldn't believe what this Mediterranean diet did to me. The pasta, the cheeses, the wine, and the countless hours sitting on my assets in the car shrank my pants. And the wallet, no matter how frugal we've been.

But it is what it is. For now, our home is the journey.

42

BEAUTIFUL UMBRIA

UMBRIA, Tuscany's little sister, lives just south of the wine-famous hills of Montepulciano, Montalcino, Cortona, and Pienza. Tuscany's shadow looms large above it, so most tourists flock to Tuscany, leaving Umbria to the connoisseurs.

Umbria is just like Tuscany without the PR. Velvety hills covered in vines and olive trees line up as far as the eye can see. Lone palatial stone houses hide behind long driveways shaded by dark cypresses that flutter in the wind like giant feathers. Narrow roads, each turn a hairpin, slow you down to 20 kilometers an hour. On top of the hills, old stone houses stand shoulder to shoulder like soldiers, making the hill towns into fortresses. Even the cemeteries here are fortresses. The cities of the dead are orderly clusters of monuments where entire families spend eternity in their ten-floor villas, each nested in his own labeled shelf.

Unsmiling porcelain faces stare you down, unaware they've been dead for years, and it's time to chill. The live ones bring flowers and candles to appease them, but it's clearly not working. They should try wine instead.

Still, despite all the human activity, Umbria's wild side is alive and kicking.

The *Fiume Tevere*, the Tiber River, slithers between hills down below. Here in Umbria, Rome's majestic river is just a milky-blue stream flowing south. Tall pines and brown oaks shade spiny blackberries and tangled rosehip bushes. Neurotic truffle-hunting dogs bark maniacally from every *agriturismo*. Pedestrians in orange vests carry rifles since the truffle-rich forests teem with deer, boar, and hare, enough of them to grace the menu of every restaurant.

This morning we took a late start toward Asissi of St. Francis fame. Then Steve took a right turn when Gwendolyn said left. He often does — that's why she sulks and stops talking to him for hours. We found ourselves heading up a lovely hill, then another. By noon, we were still a good hour away from Asissi. We needed lunch, and we had to shop for dinner since here, in the middle of nowhere, there's no food for miles. Unless you graze.

We ditched Assisi for the nearby village of Todi. I went shopping while Steve stayed in the car and burned up our data, checking the news on the phone. I got bread, eggs, coffee, and a *lepere* — rabbit — ready to cook. I couldn't resist a *cotechino fresco*, a log-shaped item as thick as my arm. I didn't know what it was, but how would I find out if I didn't buy it? And it was on sale!

Time for lunch. I checked Trip Advisor and directed Steve to a well-reviewed restaurant 10 kilometers away. Barely half an hour on those hills.

Steve was skeptical. Half the time, when we look for a restaurant, we check with Mr. Google to make sure it's open, and we find it closed.

Not this one. They checked our green passes and sat us at

the table by the fire. We sipped on a nice red — we're still learning the Umbrian wines — and checked the menu.

"How about the bruschetta with lard?" Steve asked.

I shivered.

Usually, bruschetta is a slice of toasted bread loaded with chopped tomatoes doused in olive oil and flavored with garlic and herbs. I couldn't see lard fitting in that picture.

"Are you sure?"

"I really feel like it."

What can you say? It's his stomach, not mine, so I moved on. Since my pants felt tight, I skipped the primo and ordered the wine-cooked deer with pomegranates. Steve chose the spaghetti carbonara with *guanciale* — pork cheek. We sipped on our wine, admiring the rather quaint decorations featuring empty Marlboro packages and reading the famous quotes written in chalk on the black walls.

"*Siamo tutti mortali fino al primo bacio e al secondo bicchiere di vino!*" We all are mortal until the first kiss and the second glass of wine.

Eduardo Hughes Galeano. Whoever he is, what a wise man!

"*E dove non e vino non e amore ne alcun altro diletto hanno i mortali.*" And where there's no wine, there's no love nor any other mortal delight." Euripides.

The amuse-bouche — a tiny crispy toast topped with an over-easy quail egg — was delicious. But then the bruschetta...

I stared at the two glassy slices of bread topped with translucent warm fat, and I shivered. Their only redeeming feature was the rosemary sprig on top.

Not enough.

Steve poked it with his fork.

"That's not what I had in mind."

I bet.

I struggled to cut a tiny taste, but the fat stretched, and the bread crumbled. I eventually managed to get a piece and put it in my mouth.

Crap.

I didn't want to be rude and spit it out, so I chewed and chewed, then washed it down with a gulp of acid wine. Then another.

I pushed away the plate and watched Steve struggle. He finished one slice and started on the next. I worried about his health.

"How about a doggy bag?" I asked.

He stared at me like I was nuts.

"You want to take this home?"

"I don't want to insult them. And I know someone who might enjoy it."

His eyes lit up.

"Spritz. Good idea."

My deer with pomegranates was flavorful and so lean it almost made up for the bruschetta. Steve's carbonara with guanciale was a bit too heavy after that lard, so I gave it a pass. We declined dessert and coffee and asked for the bill. The owner brought it along with a whole bottle of green pistachio liquor and two glasses.

"Enjoy. On the house."

The milky sweet drink slid down like silk. I had to wrestle it away from Steve — after all, he was driving — but that came just in time to illustrate what I was telling him.

"Let's not rush through Italy to get to Spain. These people want you. They are genuine, friendly, and hospitable, not only chasing your wallet. Italy is a good place to be."

"And Spain isn't?"

I don't know. I've been prejudiced since that time in Barcelona ten years ago when I fell by the crowded *La Sagrada Familia* cathedral. I twisted my ankle so bad that I couldn't stand, but nobody came to help. A hundred people stared at me, watching me struggle to get up, then limp away. It was downright weird. That soured me on Spain.

But maybe they weren't Spaniards and Christians, just tourists. Or they were busy. Or something. I shrugged.

"Who knows? But isn't Italy wonderful? Let's make the most of it.

43

ASSISI

WE SPENT most of our time at the farm convalescing, watching Maria work while we lazed around, making fires from the olive trimmings, and looking for food since the eating establishments were few and far between. Still, we managed a trip to Assisi.

Unlike its wine-famous neighbors, the town of Assisi's fame comes from its best son, St. Francis, the patron saint of Italy whose name Pope Francis took. Francis's message of love, humility, and poverty conquered people's souls. It gave them faith and hope in a time when the power of the church manifested in ostentatious wealth.

Francis, the handsome son of a wealthy silk merchant — the medieval equivalent of being born a Gucci — lived the good life and enjoyed the pleasures of the flesh until he went to war. He was taken prisoner, and a year later, the experience brought him back a changed man.

In a public display immortalized in his cathedral's murals, Francis gave up all worldly riches, ripped off his silk clothes and threw them at his father, then ran away naked.

I hope it wasn't in winter.

He commandeered some itchy horsehair garment from a

peasant, tied it with a rope instead of his rich belt complete with moneybag and weapons, and made a vow of poverty. He chose to live like a penitent, praying, begging, restoring dilapidated old chapels, and caring for the lepers.

He preached God's love to whoever would listen, from people to birds.

People listened. Before long, other idealistic young men, inspired by his ideas, followed in his steps. Thus, the Franciscan order of the Fratelli Minori was born.

Women soon followed. Saint Clare, a young noblewoman, ran away from home. She renounced her family and bright future to live in faith and poverty and started a women's movement — the order of the Poor Clares.

Remember that this all happened in the thirteenth century when the Catholic church's wealth was immeasurable and its power immense. Whoever didn't align with the church party line risked excommunication and a gruesome death.

But, thanks to God, or maybe Pope Innocent III's enlightened confessor, the pope condoned this movement instead of feeding it to the inquisition. Francis and his followers started an order aiming to follow Christ's teachings and walk in his footsteps. Their message of faith, love, and humility spread like wildfire.

Thus came the fame of Assisi.

Today's entire Assisi is a monument to Saint Francis. Church after church celebrates his deeds and ideals, and every bar in Assisi bears his name. As you walk from one Nativity scene to another, the narrow streets are lined with shops selling all things Saint Francis.

From elaborate rosaries to St. Francis statues; from tote bags bearing his portrait to glass-painted Basilicas and wooden crucifixes carved with his name; from lavender pouches with his image to stuffed purple rabbits named Francis, everything in

Assisi is about St. Francis — and your money. Every church, store, and drinking hole in Assisi is hell-bent on helping you reach St. Francis's ideal of renunciation and poverty. That's why the place has more ATMs per mile than anywhere I've ever been.

It was freezing as we walked down the decorated streets to the majestic Basilica. We shivered, pulled our raincoats closer, and lined up behind the other hundreds of faithful to see St. Francis's tomb.

We discovered there are actually two basilicas on top of each other. Three, if you count the underground crypt sheltering Saint Francis's humble tomb amongst countless riches.

The holy men of the church herded us at a steady clip down the corridors, by the tomb, then back up the stairs to keep the flow of the faithful going. And their donations.

We ended at the life-sized and very diverse Nativity scene in front of the Basilica. The onlookers were brown, Joseph was black, and the cow and the mule warming Baby Jesus with their breaths couldn't be more delighted.

We left Assisi in wonder. How could this idealistic humble man leave such a profound mark on the world and still not change it at all?

44

CIVITA DI BAGNOREGIO

THE FIRST TIME we tried to see Civita, we didn't make it. It was just an hour's drive from our farm, but we kept pulling over for pictures, then we finally found a pharmacy and stopped to get something for my mangled knee.

Three days later, it's still dressed in honey and duct tape, and it's not looking pretty. That doesn't bother me since I have better things to do than look at my knees, but it hurts like the dickens every time I bend it to get in the car, climb stairs, or even walk. So, when we finally saw the green cross of a pharmacy, we stopped for supplies.

I hobbled up the stairs into what looked like a meeting in front of the door. It turns out it was just the queue. Due to Covid, they only allowed one person inside at a time. By the way, people in Italy don't queue like we do. People don't line up — why should they? How could they talk if they couldn't see each other's hands? They circle instead, but everyone knows when it's their turn.

So I circled to wait with the others and watched the conversation, but I was anxious. How will I know when it's my turn?

Nessun problema. No problem. Six customers later,

everyone turned to stare at me when someone came out. Sharp as I am, I immediately figured I was next, so I limped in.

I asked for a bandage. The pharmacist couldn't find them. He looked on the shelves, went to the back room, checked the drawers, and peeped under the counter. Nothing. He called his partner, who suggested he check the fridge. Sadly, they weren't there either.

Twenty minutes later, I left with a small tube of antibiotic ointment. The circle by the door had doubled, and they all glared at me, wondering what had taken me so long.

Since my Italian wasn't good enough to explain about the fridge and all, I just shrank and hobbled back to the car. Still, by the time we finally got to Bagnoregio, it was too late, so we aborted our mission and planned to return. We did it on our way to Tuscany.

We snuck through Bagnoregio's narrow streets — you sense a motif here, don't you — to the parking lot nearest Civita. Civita doesn't do cars, and my knee was still on strike. We bought tickets — you need to pay to visit Civita, like you would for a museum, and rightly so because Civita is a museum. It's the live museum of a dead city.

Perched on a high rocky outcrop and connected to Bagnoregio by a long pedestrian bridge, Civita has been dying for years. Like a man sick with lepers dropping fingers here and there, Civita has been losing piece after piece of herself to the abyss below. Gardens, walls, roads, and whole buildings fell off the cliff, leaving striking ruins behind. A lone wall here, sporting a window framing the mountains, a broken spiral stair to nowhere, a street sign toward thin air.

It's striking but strangely not sad.

Maybe because it was a glorious day. A bright sun kissed the honey-colored buildings, the colorful gardens, and the magnificent landscape below, making the place feel joyous, despite the herds of tourists clogging the streets.

We wandered down the *vicolos*, the narrow alleys crossing the half-mile of the main road still left. We stopped at the *Giardina Del Poete*, the Poet's garden, a lovely garden perched over the abyss. It belongs to two young men who scratch a living by allowing people to visit. They let you in to take photos in exchange for buying something from their *prodotti tipici* store that sells pasta, beans, fruit preserves, and olive oil.

I hobbled around the magic garden, taking pictures of everything, from Steve to their cat. I knew I was somewhere I'd never forget: The golden light, the breathtaking mountains miles away, and the care they'd put into making the place charming, though it would soon get swallowed by the abyss below.

This place and this moment will never return. I felt it in my bones. Unlike feeling awed by eternity, I had a brush with temporality. I felt deeply aware of the fleeting moment and my mortality.

But for now, we're still here. *Carpe diem.*

I looked for something to buy, but they had nothing we needed, so I left a well-received tip. They loved it, but my thanks lit up their faces.

"What a magic place you created! Thank you for giving me wonderful memories."

We made it back to the car just as the parking meter expired. We were tired and frozen, but our hearts were full of joy, and we were grateful to have been there.

45

TUSCANY

I DECIDED I wouldn't like Tuscany. Everyone else did, and the hype was getting on my nerves. Tuscany this, Tuscany that — Tuscan cuisine, Tuscan wines, Tuscany's landscapes, Tuscan hill towns, art, culture, whatever. I decided it was just an over-hyped version of Umbria with better PR.

Frances Mayes' overblown *Under the Tuscan Sun* got turned into a movie everyone pretends to have seen. A couple more books primed the American tourist market and whipped the demand into a frenzy. That built up the supply, rekindled the PR, which rebuilt the demand, and so on. There couldn't be much more to Tuscany than to lovely Umbria, could there? It was all hype. So, when we left Maria, Spritz, and Leonardo, I was determined to be unimpressed.

It turns out I wasn't all wrong. Tuscany isn't necessarily better than Umbria. It has the same velvety green hills covered with vines and olive trees. The same hilltop towns with old stone houses hugging together like old maids in church. The same graceful cedar-shaded driveways and honey-colored stone houses build to last. The same fluffy clouds chase each other over shifty skies, throwing fast-moving shadows over the ground below. Other than its head-turning wines with mouthwatering names like Nobile de Montepulciano, Brunello de Montalcino, and Rosso de Cortona, Tuscany isn't any better than Umbria.

But it's beautiful!

I resisted her for the five minutes it took us to get from the highway to the back roads, and I got hooked. By the time we reached our sunny home in Montepulciano, a spacious apartment on the edge of town fitted with everything one could hope for and perfectly triangulated between a *pasticeria*, a bar-pizzeria, and a supermarket, I'd forgotten Umbria like I forgot last winter's snow.

Our charming host Elias, a kick-ass environmentalist specializing in Brazilian martial arts, helped us settle. One day later, we no longer wanted to leave.

Day one was lovely and sunny, so we wandered up and down Montepulciano's pedestrian-friendly narrow streets. We window-shopped stylish boutiques of many kinds, all hell-bent on lightening your wallet.

The first product here is wine, of course, but there's so much more. And I'm not talking fridge magnets and cheap souvenirs. Not much here is cheap, by the way.

There are fashions, from cashmere coats and silk scarves to long-sleeved K-9 hoodies. And if you think dogs don't care about fashion, think again. K-9 envy is something to behold. More than once, I've watched naked dogs bark furiously at their elegant counterparts who look at them down their long noses.

The Italian greyhound sporting a body-hugging royal purple turtleneck reminded me of Paris Hilton. She had nothing but scorn for the naked hairy pointer looking like Judy Dench, who barked up a storm.

"Look at you! Hussy! Is that a way for a decent dog to dress?" Judy growled.

Paris shrugged.

"Like you have room to talk. Did you even notice you're naked?"

Judy got so mad she charged to rip off Paris's coat, but her human dragged her away. Paris watched her leave with an arrogant smirk before shaking her stuff on her way to some runway somewhere.

There are leather stores where Italian craftsmen turn animal hides into all things leather, from custom-made boots to purses, jackets, gloves, and aprons. Forged iron stores where garden sculptures rub shoulders with chandeliers, house numbers, and solar clocks. Bright ceramics where Tuscany's green sets off Sorrento's lemon-yellow. Purple shops, with everything lavender, from the potpourri and sachets to hand creams and lavender-scented purple bunnies. There are artistic bookbinders, a profession that I thought was extinct. Wood shops, where the smooth, grained olive wood turns into cutting boards, trivets, salad bowls, and cooking utensils too beautiful to use. The ubiquitous *antichi sapori* (traditional flavors) stores burst with olive oil, wine, cheeses, artisanal pastas, and limoncello. Not to mention the restaurants, bars, and cafés.

Montepulciano is shamelessly seductive. It confidently puts it all there: breathtaking landscapes, beautiful houses, and rich offerings. One can't but lust, so I drooled my way from one window shop to the next.

But our suitcases were full, and we were sort of homeless, so we bought nothing other than what we ate or drank. But we did it with gusto.

Our first stop was the *enoteca*, the ultra-modern establishment at the town's top. It's built on top of a thousand-year-old Etruscan ruins that you can see through the plexiglass floors as you sip your wine.

The large room flooded with light is sparsely furnished. It

looks like a fast-food joint, but for the futuristic wine-tasting machines living on its walls. Locked glass refrigerators hold bottles of Rosso and Nobile de Montepulciano there for the tasting. You buy a card from the bar, grab a glass, choose a wine, slide in the card, and push a button to have the AI waiter serve you 33 milliliters of wine. Sniff, smell, taste, and repeat.

That was a wine tasting like we've never had, though we've tasted many wines over five continents. It was a triumph of modern technology and unencumbered personal choice.

I'm all for personal choice. I hate being helped — from trying on shoes to having food, I'd rather do it myself — but Steve didn't like it. He didn't mind the wine, but the process put him off, and I know why.

Years ago, before Covid, when meeting people was still a thing, we were in the lovely Canadian village of Niagara on the Lake. We spent a pleasant hour tasting and talking wines with the charming oenologist at the Stratus vineyards. I can't remember his name, but I can remember his warmth, enthusiasm, and knowledge of all things wine. We had a precious time I'll never forget. But this wine-dispensing machine? Not so much.

We headed back along the winding lanes to look for lunch. We found a pizza joint near Piazza Grande, where we had our first *pizza degustation*.

The first course was a pizza Margherita that could be the best pizza I've ever had. The prettiest, too, with lumpy balls of snow-white Mozzarella nestled in fragrant red tomato sauce sprinkled with bright-green basil pesto.

The second was a fried seafood pizza. That was interesting. Not bad, mind you, other than the anchovies — there's fish, and then there are anchovies. They live in a class of their own. They were not as bad as the squid, though. I'm still wearing its ink, and I probably will forever since nothing but scissors will get it out of my pants.

The third dish was the super-fermented pizza. The dough had been fermented for thirty-six hours and tasted like yesterday's beer. All I can say is that there is such a thing as too much of a good thing.

We were just about to finish when two armed *carabinieri* stopped by our table asking to see our IDs and health passes.

To combat this umpteenth wave of Covid, Italy mandated the vaccine for everyone over fifty. Masks are mandatory, inside and out, and the vaccination center down the road has people queuing outside. But checking your vaccination status while having lunch? That's a first!

46

EATING IN TUSCANY

EATING in Tuscany is always an experience. Not because of the food — the food is always fantastic, and the wine washing it down is stupendous. But it's not about the food. It's about the people.

I told you about the pizza tasting. That was just the beginning.

Two days ago, we decided to take the trip to Montalcino — for those who don't know, that's like Bethlehem for wine worshipers. If you've never heard of Brunello di Montalcino, Google it. It's Montalcino's aged brown wine, and it's famous worldwide. Its younger brother Rosso is lovely too, and way less expensive. But for me, Brunello is where it's at.

It must have been 20 years ago that Steve and I visited Rome. For some reason — probably a sale — we stayed at Albergo Del Senato, a posh hotel right across from the Pantheon. The hotel was beautiful, and the view was stunning, but the tuxedoed doorman made me feel like a slob. Well deserved, too, since I travel like one — no makeup, no jewelry, no high-heels. Often not even clean clothes. But, in that hotel, I felt like I didn't belong, so I avoided the door like the plague.

I'd have jumped out the window if I could, but it was on the second floor.

One day we went out and soaked in the marvels of Rome. We got back after a lovely lunch that may have involved wine. We lay for a nap and woke to the moon dripping silver over the Pantheon's dome. It was close to midnight, and I was so hungry the cotton towels looked tasty.

Now what?

We could brave the doorman and go out, looking for an open *trattoria*. Or we could make do.

I rummaged through our luggage, but I didn't find much other than dirty socks, yesterday's lunch sandwiches that didn't look good at the time, and a bottle of expensive Brunello I had bought for Steve's ex-wife. Steve thought I was crazy to spend 50 euros on a bottle of wine, but I owed my sister-wife a debt of gratitude. But that's another story for another time.

Go out or stay in?

I glanced at the stale sandwiches, then at the Brunello.

I'll buy her another.

We stayed in. Steve opened the Brunello with his handy knife and poured it into our plastic teeth-brushing glasses. We sipped on it, sitting on the windowsill, watching the moon set behind the Pantheon, and munching on stale sandwiches.

I've never had a sandwich taste so good. And that night, two decades ago? It was so magical I wrote it in one of my thrillers. All thanks to that Brunello.

That's why I love Brunello. I like Bordeaux and Marlborough Sauvignon Blancs, and I just discovered the Salice Salentino. But Brunello? There's nothing like it. That's why being in Montalcino is almost a pilgrimage.

We were frozen and hungry by the time we got to Montalcino. We parked outside the town, as usual, since Italian cities welcome you, but not your car.

Steve commanded a parking spot, and I went to pay.

Surprise, surprise: No cards, no banknotes. Only coins.

I had no coins. I'd left them at home.

We headed back hungry. We ended up on a steep, unpaved road that couldn't be the way out of the home of the most famous wines in the world. Could it?

It was.

Steve maneuvered between vines, olive groves, and pastures, squeezing the Citroën between unforgiving stone walls and steep ravines. Here and there, horses stared at us like we were nuts. Geese hissed. People frowned.

We went on.

It took us a while to figure out that we were driving the *Via Francigena*, the ancient way of the pilgrims from Canterbury to Apulia via Rome that the crusaders used to take. But now that the crusades are few and far between, *Via Francigena* has fallen into disrepair. It lost most of its pilgrims to the Camino De Santiago, which has better PR and facilities.

Still, we were hungry. Fortunately, we found a "Pilgrim's Café" in the nearby village of Torrigiani.

"*Pranzo?*" Lunch? I asked.

The woman at the counter shook her head.

"*Solo panini.*" Only sandwiches.

We needed more for our one meal of the day, so we shuffled toward the door when an elderly woman waved to get my attention.

"The *osteria*. Down there, then right," she said in sign language.

"I'll show them." A man came out to direct us.

"Go down there. *No primo. Segundo.*" Not the first, but the second.

The second what?

He saw my puzzlement.

"*Primo, no. Segundo, si,*" he said helpfully, sliding his right thumb up his cheek in the Italian sign for "*delizioso,*" delicious.

I thanked him profusely and got in the car.

"What did he say?" Steve asked.

"I don't know. Something like down there, but not the first one, the second."

"The second what?"

"Maybe street?"

We headed down. A hundred feet later, we saw the sign for *Cantina,* restaurant, to our right. But...

"There, down there."

The *Osteria* was the second *trattoria* on the street. And it was *delizioso*! The *pappardelle all sugo* were scrumptious, the wine was smooth and cheap, and the hosts were charming.

It wasn't Montalcino, but what a lunch!

But we couldn't leave Tuscany without giving Montalcino another try, so we went to the supermarket to secure coins.

Steve bought two oranges worth two euros with a twenty. I bought a red pepper worth one euro with another.

The cashier was not amused.

"One euro?" she said.

I shrugged and handed her the twenty.

She shook her head until her false lashes fell off, then counted my change. As she shot me another wilting glare, we were already on our way to Montalcino with our pockets heavy with coins, all set to park. Then, when we got there, I discovered that the parking meter took cards. Go figure!

We left the car and worked our way up the steep, cobbled lanes. They were empty. Like, postapocalyptic empty. Nothing moved as far as the eye could see but the few plumes of smoke coming out the chimneys.

We pulled our coats closer and braved the sharp wind that

brought tears to my eyes and numbed my fingers into sticks. I hadn't been so cold since Belize, but that's yet another story.

We wandered through one empty street after another, wondering where everyone had gone. We sheltered from the wind behind the church atop the hill to wonder at the incredible landscape below. I took two pictures before my fingers froze, and I almost dropped my iPhone into the abyss.

We'd been in Montalcino for all of twenty minutes, and we were about to succumb to hypothermia. We needed to shelter fast, but it wasn't noon yet, and nothing looked open except the frozen church.

The first bar was closed. So was the second. So was the *enoteca*, with its sun-bleached advertising posters flapping in the wind.

But look! An Osteria! I tried the door, and it opened. We scrambled in, inhaling the ambrosial aromas of pasta and meat.

The hallway was empty, but a table of twelve was loaded with steamy, mouth-watering platters and packed with people. Now you're talking! I ogled them with hope. They stared back.

"Yes?" a white-aproned man said.

I swallowed my drool, then noticed their white caps and aprons. They weren't customers. It was the staff having lunch family-style before they opened.

"We'll be back," I said.

It was only a quarter to noon, but I didn't have another fifteen minutes of freezing left in me. Luckily, the bar across the street was open. We rushed in.

The place wasn't fancy. A modest affair with small wooden tables, a coffee machine, and shelves heavy with pastries. But the wall behind the counter was nothing but wines.

I waited as a customer got his cappuccino, then begged the gray-haired lady behind the counter.

"*Vino? Due becchieri?*" Wine? Two glasses?"

I knew she'd tell me it wasn't noon yet, so there was no wine. But this wasn't America.

"Brunello or Rosso?"

"Brunello."

"Go sit," she motioned. Or something to that effect. I grabbed a table as Steve went to look for the bathroom. It was locked.

He went to get the key but got asked for the green pass. You can't even pee in Italy unless you're vaccinated, I thought, watching Steve chat with the lady. That took a long time. But I wasn't worried since Steve's Italian is even worse than mine.

I was wrong.

"There's something wrong with our passes," he said.

"What?"

"I don't know. She kept saying something, then pointed to the ham. I said no. But she started cutting bread."

He returned from the bathroom just as the lady brought two glasses of Brunello and a plate loaded with mouth-watering prosciutto sandwiches.

We thanked her and tried the wine.

One was a lovely 2015 Verbena Brunello. The other was a 2016 Catiguano. Both stupendous.

We ordered more.

When we left, we were no longer cold. We'd had enough to eat and drink, so we skipped lunch and went home. But what lovely, hospitable people! To Italy!

47

THE HUMAN CONNECTION

BUT THERE'S MORE to restaurants than food or even wine. Here in Italy, more than anywhere else, today's restaurants do what churches used to do: Bring people together.

Two days ago, after another freezing stroll around Montepulciano's empty streets — a shocker after the lively crowds on the weekend — we found ourselves by *Osteria del Conte*, a traditional restaurant just off Piazza Grande. As usual, we were frozen and hungry, so we went in.

It wasn't big — just ten tables or so, most of them for two, none taken. We asked for the table in the corner, but they said no. It was reserved.

So we sat elsewhere and started fighting with the QR code to get the menu.

I'd just ordered half a liter of the house wine (a decision I would come to regret) as two *anziani* (senior citizens) came in. The waitress greeted them like long-lost friends and helped them to the table we were denied.

They took off their hats and winter jackets and sat facing each other. The one by the wall was tall and bald, with sharp eyes and rimless glasses. His partner was smaller, with gray hair arranged into an artful combover and hands that never stood still.

A half-carafe of wine arrived before they got to sit. The *antipasti* followed. They started eating, and I lost track of them to watch an arriving young lady.

An old lady came out of the kitchen. She wiped her hands on her apron, and they hugged and kissed like a grandmother and granddaughter would. They sat, and a bottle of wine came out of nowhere. The pasta followed.

I checked back on the *anziani*. They'd finished the antipasti and moved on to *ravioli al sugo* sprinkled with cheese. They were so comfortable with each other that they didn't speak much.

Grandma went back to the kitchen, and a well-dressed man with a hot pink scarf carrying a bowl of salad took her seat. He poured himself some wine, then chopped some *finocchio* — anise — in the salad while checking his ledgers.

Two good-looking Eurasian men in their thirties sat at the table by the door. They ordered wine, then became engrossed in an intense conversation I struggled to eavesdrop on. Looking at their matching bracelets and wedding bands, I wondered if they talked about their wedding or divorce.

The *anziani* finished their *primi* and dug into some upside-down cheese-covered cupcakes. Pink scarf left, and the waitress took his seat. The two men continued their heated conversation as their food got cold.

Steve kicked me.

"Eat," he said, pointing to my tripe congealing under a layer of grated cheese that covered it like snow. I'd never had cheese on my tripe before, but the waitress said I should, so who was I to disagree? I started eating, keeping an eye on the action, and wishing they had subtitles.

The *anziani* finished their strange *secondi* and moved on to their fruit. Grandma came back to say goodbye. The men finished their wine, but not the conversation. They ordered more — wine, that is. The young woman hugged grandma and left.

Then something happened.

The tall *anziano* pulled out a ten-euro note, set it on the table, and covered it with his watch. The short one got out his wallet. They paid, donned their coats, and shuffled toward the door.

The waitress waved.

"See you tomorrow," the short one said.

I was mesmerized.

Who are they? Brothers? Friends? They didn't act like lovers, and they each paid their share. They didn't speak much, and they didn't look excited to meet. Do they come here every day?

So many questions, so few answers.

We paid our bill. The two young men gazed into each other's eyes as we left.

Wedding, I thought. Definitely not divorce. Though…

"We have to come back," I said.

Steve laughed.

"Tomorrow?"

"Yes. I need to know if they come here every day."

But the next day, we got busy freezing our assets in Montalcino and didn't make it.

But today…

We stepped in at a quarter to one. The place was almost full. Sitting at her usual seat, the young woman chatted with grandma. The two young men were missing.

But at the table in the corner, the two *anziani* were working on their wine.

They finished their *primi* and started their *secondi*.

They peeled their clementines and ate their grapes.

The tall one removed his watch and set it on the table on top of a ten-euro note. The short one took out his wallet.

As they left, he brushed against our table. He smiled at me.

"Buona giornata," he said. Have a good day.

"Anche a lei." You too.

48

ITALY'S HILL TOWNS

As our time in Italy approached its end, we hopped from one charming place to another, wishing we could stay forever. And every one of the hill towns gave us reasons to linger.

Speaking about Italy's hill towns is a bit of an oxymoron. They all are, since every Italian hill wears a village on its top like a hat. Stone houses stick together like a gang of teenagers who know they're in trouble since they're late for curfew.

Everywhere else I've been, from Norway to Patagonia, people built their homes along the water. That's how cities came to be, from London and Paris to villages you've never heard about. Not here.

Whether it's the fear of floods or the dread of invaders, Italians love to build on hilltops, even if that means carting up the water.

It started even before ancient Rome with the Etruscans. Then, when Rome fell to the herds of barbarian invaders, people gravitated to the hills, building and fortifying even more towns that would eventually become independent city-states. The last remaining one is San Marino.

That may be why Italy's hill towns managed to keep their unique individuality and flavor. From Cortona's wine, Volterra's ruins, and San Gimignano's stair-like streets to Pisa's drunk tower and Lucca's fortified walls you could drive a monster truck on, each town has a unique history, identity, and culture.

That may also be why it took Italy longer than most other European countries to get itself together and become a state. But finally, on March 17, 1861, the *Risorgimento*, Garibaldi's unification movement, unified the independent and often rival Italian cities under the same flag and gave birth to Italy, the cradle of pizza, gelato, Mafia, La Dolce Vita, and Sergio Leone's spaghetti westerns.

On our way north, we stopped in Siena, a charming place that basks in its past glory and is home to the world's oldest bank, *Banca Monte dei Paschi di Siena*, operating since the fifteenth century. Long ago, Siena was a prosperous city the size of medieval Paris. For centuries, it wrestled Florence for supremacy. That may be why it's so steeped in the past.

Siena's narrow cobblestoned streets haven't changed in centuries. Any moment you'd expect a Roman chariot to whizz by. Even worse, the parking spaces stayed the same. So we parked outside the city and meandered in.

As we got there, Piazza del Campo, the heart of the town, basked in the morning sun. It was quaint and quiet, like you'd expect with Covid and the winter when the tourists were almost extinct. But twice a year, Siena recovers its former glory. That's when the *Palio di Siena*, Italy's most famous horse race, takes over the downtown.

Twice each summer, the city prepares for the event. The stone walls get padded to shield the riders, and the cobblestones get covered with clay to protect the horses' hooves. Then the best horses in the city, representing ten of its eighteen neighborhoods, race for glory and the *Palio*, a painted banner with the image of the Virgin Mary.

It's a no-holds-barred, winner-takes-all, bareback race. The winner is not the first jockey but the first horse, whether it still has a jockey or not. To everyone else's envy, the winning neighborhood gets to display the *Palio* until the next crazy race. And crazy it is. Just watching a replay of it on one of the outdoor monitors got our blood boiling.

We walked the streets and gawked at Siena's unfinished cathedral. It's humongous, even though it's barely a tiny piece of what it was meant to be. Fueled by pride more than faith, the Sienese planned to erect the largest cathedral ever built in Tuscany. They set up the massive columns meant to hold up a dome more impressive than that of Florence. The building was well on its way when the Black Death struck Tuscany, killing a third of Siena.

"God's work!" the faithful said. "He's punishing us for our pride."

The Sienese cried, prayed, and repented, then closed the newly built nave. They made it into today's cathedral and abandoned the rest.

Today's cathedral is a massive and very ornate piece of work guarded by Siena's symbol, which happens to also be Rome's — the she-wolf with Romulus and Remus. Looking forlorn and embarrassed, a few gigantic columns hide within the walls of today's police station, a hundred feet away. That, and a couple of humongous windows toward nowhere, are all that's left of their grandiose plan.

We lingered in *Piazza del Campo* to bask in the sun and watch the pigeons bathe in the Fountain of Joy, the first fountain to bring free water via an aqueduct. We marveled at the grandiose city hall whose tower, taller than the churches, dominates the town. That's meant to remind everyone that Italy is a secular state and the people's democracy trumps the church any day of the week.

We stopped at a classy restaurant built on top of an Etruscan tomb like most Sienese buildings are and wondered if its crumbling roof held up by rough poles would interrupt our lunch. But it didn't. We got through our wild boar dish accompanied by a plate of braided sliced raw carrots. We gawked at the deconstructed tiramisu that looked like it had already been eaten once. We gasped at the bill. But the roof stayed put, so we headed to Volterra.

Volterra was lovely but not as exciting as certain vampire movies make it look. We scoured the back streets, looking for shifters. We only found one: the lonely stuffed werewolf guarding the torture museum. Its long yellow fangs and burning eyes make it look ferocious, but its chiseled chest got worn by the furtive caresses of his many fans.

I took pictures of the horrid torture tools for my upcoming book about Vlad the Impaler, the inspiration for Bram Stoker's *Dracula*. Those instruments were real and horrendous. If that's something you are interested in, the Volterra torture museum is the place to go.

We escaped the dungeon to lunch and window shop, crossed the crowded market without buying a thing, then marveled at all things alabaster, from statues to lamps, in every shop window.

Frozen and tired, we returned to our temporary home to decide what to do.

It's mid-January, and it gets colder every day. I raided a local flea market and bought us secondhand coats, gloves, and hats for the price of a mediocre dinner, but we're not winter-ready. We have no boots or warm socks, my only sweater has grown holes from too much washing, and Steve's down hoodie smells like it died long ago.

The car isn't winter-ready, either. It has summer tires and no chains, though every place we drive into requires them.

We decided to skip Lake Cuomo and the Dolomites, which are even further north and therefore colder, and cross into Southern France, then Spain. After two months of exploring Italy from Sardinia and Sicily to here, we'll say *arrivederci* and move on.

49

LEAVING ITALY

It was a lovely bright day the morning we left Italy, but our hearts were heavy with doom. And, like a jilted lover putting on her finest to show you what you've lost, Italy decked herself to the nines. It shamelessly put it all out there — a bright sunrise gilding the stone buildings overlooking the Mediterranean, a shimmering sea, jagged dark mountains guarding the highway, and tunnel after tunnel after tunnel — there must have been a hundred — each opening to yet another spectacular view of the Italian Riviera as we sped toward France.

How could you not succumb to her charms?

"I wouldn't mind a place up here," Steve said, after three months through Europe in which he never spoke of anything but buying boats. And cars.

"Really?"

"It's pretty. And it looks livable."

It sure did. We took note of the town — it's called Imperia, and it congratulates itself for having the best climate in Italy — and started wondering how we could return.

"What is it about Italy that feels so good?" I asked Steve.

He shrugged.

"I don't know. Maybe because it doesn't put on airs?"

That's true. Unlike many places that shall remain unnamed, Italy doesn't put on airs. Italy is the country equivalent of the girl next door — pretty, unpretentious, and easy to love.

"The food isn't bad either. As for the wine…"

No need to say more. We sampled Italy's wines like we were on a mission — maybe because we were. We have our favorites, some of them we never tried before, but there aren't many slouches. As much as I love Thailand, its wines, mostly imported and ten times more expensive, don't hold a candle to Italy's five-euro carafes of house wines.

"Not warm, though."

Steve nodded.

This was our biggest disappointment. Coming from upstate New York, where we count our minuses in Fahrenheit like trophies, we expected Italy to be, if not swimsuit worthy, at least balmy. And it was not.

Truth be told, even though it's January, we've had a few lucky lunches in the sun. We sat on cozy terraces shielded from the wind and watched the sea shimmer while sipping on some voluptuous red. Still, most of the time, we shivered — whether walking the streets, eating in restaurants, or hoping our space heater wouldn't blow up the antique electric circuits yet again. With some variations, Italy's winter was pretty much like upstate New York's November, minus the freezing rain. An excellent minus, I agree, but not even close to balmy.

The prices weren't bad, especially in the south. Most accommodations, usually whole apartments or at least studios, sometimes including breakfast, were less than a hundred euros per night. Eating out was affordable. Most meals for two, including a bottle of very decent wine, would set you back about 70 euros. And here, unlike in America, tips are just chump change, not a third of the bill. That's because waiters are actually paid a living wage for their work. But the gas, at about two dollars for a liter — about eight dollars per gallon — helped even out things. All in all, cheaper than home but not by much.

Covid threw in an extra wrench. Once in a while, we'd been reminded to wear our masks properly. Most of the time, we were asked for a health pass to be allowed in restaurants. We noticed the queues at vaccination centers, since Italy, like many other European countries, cracked down on Covid. Many places were closed, whether because of winter or Covid. But all in all, things went smoother than in the United States, and people seemed less angry and more ready to move on. Maybe because Italy had the first terrible experience outside China, and they haven't forgotten the frozen trucks used to supplement the morgues. Either way, Covid wasn't a huge deal for us.

The landscapes are incredible. There's never a dull moment, even on the highway. From green marshes to white-capped marble mountains, Italy has it all. I took so many pictures that my phone got heavy. I can't ever find the license plate photos we need to park, even though I put them in "Favorites" — there are thousands of them.

Italy's beauty is hard to describe and impossible to imagine. From Sardinia's forested mountains that tumble into the azure sea miles below to Palermo's chaotic markets, Agrigento's Greek temples, Lecce's ornate buildings, Montalcino's vine-yards, and Volterra's mysterious mountains, Italy has it all. And that's without going anywhere near the big cities. As much as we love them, we avoided Rome, Venice, Florence, Naples, and Milan like the plague. Driving the backwaters was hard enough.

The food? Don't even get me started! Whether you're a carnivore or a vegetarian; whether you love fish or you're allergic to seafood; and whether you have a sweet tooth or go Keto, Italy has you covered.

But what we loved most about Italy was the people. They are friendly, curious, and cool. They work hard and love life, food, and friendships in a wholly Italian way. They value the finer things in life, and they know that some things are more important than looking cool, a job, and even money. Even more than the French, whose *joie de vivre* may clash with their slightly uppity attitude, Italians enjoy *la dolce vita* like kids do: with curiosity, greed, and gusto.

Viva Italia!

ADDENDUM:

A few Italian words you'll want to know. Unsurprisingly, most of them have to do with food.

A presto: See you soon
A dopo: See you later
Adesso: Right now
Acqua: Water
Acqua frizzante: Soda water
Aiuto: Help
Amico: Friend
Amore: Love
Arancini: Deep-fried rice balls, stuffed with meat and cheese. Popular Sicilian street food.
Aperto: Open
Arrivederci: Goodbye
Arrosto: Roasted
Attento: Watch out
Baba: A sickly sweet Neapolitan desert — spongy cake soaked in sugary syrup and rum.
Bella: Beautiful

Bene: Good

Benvenuto: Welcome

Bolognese: Red pasta with meat and spices native to Bologna that's hard to find in the islands.

Bottarga: Dry mullet roe, much loved in the islands and Italy's south, that gets grated like *parmegiano* on top of many dishes. It's saltier than salt and fishier than a con man, and it takes some getting used to.

Buonanotte: Goodnight

Buongiorno: Hello

Buonasera: Good evening

Cagnulari: Aromatic, Sicilian red wine with dark fruit aromas of cherries and raspberries and floral and herbal notes.

Casa: House

Cannoli: Ricotta-filled fried pastry tubes. The good ones get filled as you wait, so they don't get soggy, and are rolled in crushed pistachios.

Carbonara: Eggy pasta with a creamy sauce flavored with pancetta.

Cassata Siciliana: Liqueur-drenched sponge cake layered with ricotta and fruit preserves, decorated with marzipan and candied fruits.

Cattivo: Bad

Cedre: Football-sized yellow citrus with a skin thicker than a rhinoceros. It's tart, but delicious with a sprinkle of sugar and a dusting of salt.

Cerasuolo di Vittoria: Sicilian red wine, the only one with a DOCG (*Denominazione di Origine Controllata*) status. It's a blend of strong-bodied *Nero d'Avola*, and fruity, light Frappato.

Chiesa: Church

Chiuso: Closed

Ciao: Bye

Cin cin: Cheers

Cinghiale: Wild boar. More common than pork in Umbria and Tuscany, often disguised as a pasta sauce.

Come ti chiami?: What's your name?

Come va?: How are you?

Coniglio in agrodolce: Rabbit in sweet and sour sauce. Traditional Sicilian dish that may include pine nuts, raisins, and chocolate.

Corposo: Voluptous. In wines: Strong-bodied.

Cotechino: Thick pork-rind sausage traditionally served for New Year's eve.

Delizioso: Delicious. Requires kissing the tips of your fingers.

Domani: Tomorrow

Falsomagro (*fake lean*): Sicilian meat dish. It looks like roast beef, but it's stuffed with *prosciutto*, cheese, and sausage stuffing rolled around hard-boiled eggs.

Granita: Sicilian semi-frozen dessert traditionally enjoyed for breakfast alongside an espresso and pastry. It's Sicily's answer to OJ.

Grappa: THE Italian spirit (as in alcohol), distilled from leftover fermented grape skins.

Grande: Big

Grazie: Thanks

Guanciale: Pork cheek. Bacon-like and not lean, but delicious.

La: There

Lepere: Wild hare

Limoncello: Lemon liquor from the Amalfi coast. It's sweet, smooth, and goes down like a fiend.

Meusa: Spleen. Not existential. The eating kind, that you'll find in a sandwich alongside cooked onions.

Mi chiamo: My name is
Mi scusi: Sorry
Minne di Sant'Agata (Saint Agata's breasts): White —
iced semispherical pastry filled with ricotta, dark choco-
late and candied fruit. The red candied cherry on top
makes it look like St. Agata's breasts that were severed
for her refusal to abandon her faith. Bon appetit!
Molti: Many
Molto: Very
Natale: Christmas
Nero d'Avola: Dense, dark Sicilian wine high in tannins
that goes with rich meat dishes.
Nessun problema: No problem. It often means: Not my
problem. Your problem.
Oggi: Today
Pancetta: Italy's answer to bacon.
Pane rustico: Crusty sourdough bread, slightly flattened
and baked in a wood-fired oven. Delicious eaten fresh
from the oven with olive oil, salt, and ground black
pepper.
Pane carasau: Paper-thin, double-baked Sardinian flat-
bread. It's so dry it can't go bad, so it used to be the
Sardinian shepherds' staple. Works better as a cracker.
Parmigiana di melanzane: Fried eggplant layered with
basil-flavored tomato sauce topped with mozzarella,
pecorino, *scamorza*, or *caciocavallo*. Cheese, in short.
Pasticeria: Pastry shop
Per favore: Please
Peperoncino: Spicy small peppers, often pickled
Peppe: Pepper
Piacere: Nice meeting you
Piccolo: Small
Piu tardi: Later

Polpette: Balls. Of the eating kind. Sometimes meat, but in Sicily they're often swordfish.

Porche?: Why?

Porcheddu: Roasted suckling pig stuffed with aromatic myrtle served on a cork tray.

Porchetta: Rolled, roasted pork belly with a thick layer of crispy skin. Delicious!

Prego: You're welcome

Quello: That

Questo: This

Qui: Here

Roletini: Rolls of meat or fish with a flavored bread-crumbs stuffing.

Ricci di mare: Sea urchins, often served with pasta. They taste like fishy foie-gras, and they're delicious!

Risotto: A cheesy rice dish that's usually watery and often undercooked. Give it a miss.

Salice Salentino: Dark purple Italian wine from Salento made from thick-skinned *Negroamaro* grapes.

Scusa: I'm sorry.

Sfincione: Oven-baked flatbread topped with oregano, anchovies, tomato sauce, and cheese. The street vendors in Palermo sell it from their three-wheeled Piaggio food trucks.

Si: Yes

Stasera: Tonight

Strada: Road

Ti amo: I love you.

Trippa: Beef tripe. It has a peculiar slimy texture and honeycomb structure that make it unmistakable. Delicious in a warm sandwich with a squeeze of lime.

Un po: A little bit

Uno: One

Addendum:

Va bene? Are you OK?
Vai via: Go away, get lost
Via: Street
Vitello: Veal. Practically, it's a retired cow. Particularly muscular in the islands.
Vino rosso: Red wine. It's usually the house wine; otherwise, it has a name.
Zuppa: Soup

AFTERWORD

Dear Reader,

Thank you for joining us on our travels. If you loved *Driving Italy*, **please leave a review** to help others find it. It means a lot to me.

Driving Italy is my love letter to France, Italy, and the wonderful Mediterranean islands. I hope it made you chuckle, but even more, I hope it inspired you to travel. I did my best, but no way can I convey the dazzling Provence colors, Corsica's cliffs feeling like the end of the world, Sardinia's peculiar charm, Sicily's utter chaos, or Italy's seduction. You should try them yourself. But what a joy!

If you want to see a few pictures, go to **RadaJones.com**. You can also sign up for updates and freebies and get in touch. I'd love to hear from you!

Be well, and have fun!

Rada

ABOUT THE AUTHOR

Rada was born in Transylvania, ten miles from Dracula's Castle. Growing up between communists and vampires taught her that humans are fickle, but you can always trust dogs and books. That's why she read every book she could get, including the phone book (too many characters, not enough action), and adopted every stray she found, from dogs to frogs.

After joining her American husband, she spent years studying medicine and working in the ER, but she still speaks like Dracula's cousin.

Rada, her husband Steve, and their dog Guinness live in a cozy Adirondack cabin ruled by a deaf black cat named Paxil. They spend their days writing, hiking, and dreaming about traveling to faraway places.

Go to **RadaJones.com** to sign up for updates and freebies.

 facebook.com/RadaJonesMD

twitter.com/JonesRada

 instagram.com/RadaJonesMD

bookbub.com/profile/rada-jones

BOOKS BY RADA JONES

BECOMING K-9: A Bomb Dog's Memoir

BIONIC BUTTER: A Three-Pawed K-9 Hero

K-9 VIPER: The Veteran's Story

LOVELY K-9: A Prison Puppy

K-9 RAMBO: The Dutch Master

K-9 PROZAK: POW

MOM: A Dog Story

OVERDOSE: An ER Psychological Thriller

MERCY: An ER Thriller

POISON: An ER Thriller

DO HARM: A Medical Thriller

STAY AWAY FROM MY ER, and Other Fun Bits of Wisdom

ER CRIMES: The Steele Files

Box Set: Books 1-3

Printed in Great Britain
by Amazon

21035083R00129